# Robert Walser Rediscovered

Drawings by Guy Davenport

# Robert Walser Rediscovered

Stories, Fairy-Tale Plays, and
Critical Responses

**Edited by Mark Harman**

Including the anti–fairy tales
**Cinderella** and **Snowwhite**
**Translated by Walter Arndt**

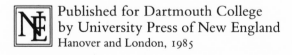
Published for Dartmouth College
by University Press of New England
Hanover and London, 1985

## University Press of New England

Acknowledgments for use of previously published materials are listed on page 219.

Printed in the United States of America

**Library of Congress Cataloging in Publication Data** ·

Walser, Robert, 1878–1956.
　　Robert Walser rediscovered.

　　Bibliography: p.
　　Includes index.
　　I. Harman, Mark.　II. Dartmouth College.　III. Title.
PT2647.A64A6　1985　　838'.91209　　84–40585
ISBN 0–87451–334–0

# Contents

# Preface

This book offers a selection of original works by Robert Walser as well as a variety of critical responses. To widen the range of Walser's writings available in English, I have included works from the early Zurich period as well as representative texts from the 1920s. The stories are arranged chronologically, followed by three short poems and the challenging Zurich fairy plays, *Cinderella* and *Snowwhite*. While the critical pieces by Walser's literary contemporaries—Walter Benjamin, Franz Kafka, and Robert Musil—offer an initial orientation, the essays by Elias Canetti and the West German novelist Martin Walser suggest the fascination that he continues to exert on present-day writers. The contributions by Walter Arndt, George Avery, Tamara Evans, Winfried Kudszus, Christopher Middleton, and myself, which grew out of a symposium held at Dartmouth College in November 1983, pursue some of the critical issues raised by Walser's work.

I should like to thank all those who, directly or indirectly, helped bring this book to life. Walter Arndt was always at hand with his polyglot advice; Peter Spycher at Oberlin gave generously of his Bernese expertise. Thanks also to Steven Scher for his encouragement, to the German Department at Dartmouth College for sponsoring the Walser symposium, and to the Max Kade Foundation and the Swiss Center Foundation for their financial support; to Dr. Elio Fröhlich and Dr. Werner Morlang of the Carl Seelig Foundation in Zurich, which houses the Robert Walser Archive; to director David Klein and cast from the Parish Players of Thetford, Vermont, who showed that Walser's *Cinderella* can captivate a New England audience; to the panelists, Sven Birketts, Laurence Davies, and Stanley Rosenberg; to the participants themselves, of course, and to Christopher Middleton in particular, who traveled to Hanover under less than ideal circumstances; and, finally, to my wife, Nina Menke, who listened to my translations with an unforgiving ear.

M. H.
*Oberlin College, Ohio*

# List of Translators

*with Key to Abbreviations*

| | |
|---|---|
| **W. A.** | Walter Arndt |
| **M. H.** | Mark Harman |
| **J. McC.** | Joseph McClinton |
| **T. W. and S. B.** | Tom Whelan and Susan Bernofsky |

# Robert Walser Rediscovered

Mark Harman

# Introduction: A Reluctant Modern

> *One day some fragrance or other will issue*
> *from my being and my beginnings . . .*
> Jakob von Gunten

Perhaps we are latecomers rather than "postmodernists." How else can we explain the widespread nostalgia for the early decades of this century? The lives of Joyce and Proust in their reincarnations at the hands of an Ellmann or a Painter captivate us, and even the memoirs of walk-on parts in the Bloomsbury saga prove irresistible. Yet, and here crusading zeal is getting the better of me, until the publication of Christopher Middleton's selection of Robert Walser's prose in 1982, with a foreword by Susan Sontag,[1] few people in English-speaking countries had ever heard of Robert Walser.

Walser is a missing link in a line of witty self-conscious writers stretching from Cervantes, Fielding, and Sterne, through Nabokov, all the way to Pynchon and Barth. Although Walser reached a large audience through the stories he published in the arts pages of newspapers, in the 1920s there was much headshaking by readers who asked: "Is it still art, what you're up to?"[2] In 1929 Walser withdrew into the asylum, that "monastery of modernity," as Elias Canetti puts it.

Walser rebelled against art in the name of life, only to find that "the will to sincerity . . . cannot satisfy itself except by aesthetic means."[3] Unlike some later practitioners of self-conscious fiction,[4] he needed writing to be more than an intricate game with language. He feared that the endless mediations of language and of literary form would overwhelm and stifle his voice. In the final story in this selection, "Sketch" (1928–29), that anguish sings in prose of brittle beauty.

Walser blends "conservative" and "avant-garde" qualities in a manner bound to strike English-speaking readers as unfamiliar, if not downright bizarre, but precedents exist in the German tradition. He shares with his nineteenth-century mentors, Swiss poetic realist Gottfried Keller (1819–90) and ironic Romantic Jean Paul (1763–1825), what J. P. Stern has called a "special combination of the prophetic and the archaic, of the existential and the parochial, of the elements of worldly innocence and reflective profundity."[5]

Before trying to suggest the role Walser's "parochial" heritage plays in his literary experiments, I should like to present a thumbnail sketch of his life. Tact is necessary in any attempt to approach Walser biographically. The protectiveness of his admirers, evident, for instance, in Canetti's broadside against opportunistic appropriations of Walser, reflects a fundamental tension running through all of Walser's writings. Walser never hid the confessional impulse behind his entire work, which he once called a "book of myself."[6] Yet he also wished to conceal himself behind the myriad of autobiographical figures gracing the pages of that book. In "The Child" (*Das Kind*), one such persona warns the reader—and would-be biographers for that matter—that "nobody is entitled to treat me as if he knew me."[7]

Born in the city of Biel in 1878, Walser was the second youngest in a large family whose fortunes never flourished. His father, by all accounts a genial individual but a hopeless businessman, first ran a fancy-goods store, and then, after it folded, made a meager living in the wine trade. Walser's mother was a woman of unpredictable moods, whose instability became so pronounced that she needed constant supervision in her final years. She died in 1894 when Robert was sixteen. In Walser's autobiographical first novel, *The Tanner Siblings* (1907), the hero's account of his relationship with his mother may suggest something of the trauma of Walser's childhood: "I had a need to be treated tenderly, and it never happened."[8]

Walser's productive life is essentially a tale of four cities: Zurich (1896–1905), Berlin (1905–13), Biel (1913–21), and Bern (1921–29). He led a nomadic life on what he described as "the periphery of bourgeois existences."[9] He was constantly changing addresses and moving from one menial clerical job to the next. When he tired of cities, he would head off on long treks through the Swiss countryside, recording many of these wanderings in seemingly effortless prose, which he rarely revised.

Walser's idiosyncratically provincial manner must have made him seem an odd apparition in the literary salons of Zurich and Berlin. Even a figure as benevolently inclined as the then famous writer Dauthendey could take him aside and advise him to change his dress so as to appear less of a "strange figure."[10] The clothes in question Walser describes as a hiking suit that had "something of southern Italy about it" and that seems to have awakened, as he puts it, more "suspicion than trust in well thought-out, well-measured Germany."[11]

The combination of Walser's irreverent sense of humor and his delight in playing roles did little to further his literary career. A Swiss publisher once received a note from Walser suggesting they meet to discuss a book project. It was signed "Caesar, servant of Mr. Walser." At the designated address, which turned out to be a dilapidated rooming house, the publisher was greeted by a tall man in shirt sleeves who mumbled something and disappeared. A few minutes later the same man entered wearing a jacket, and announced that he was Robert Walser.[12] By naming his servant persona "Caesar," Walser injects into that lowly station more than a hint of self-aggrandizement. Far from being an isolated prank, the incident reflects Walser's lifelong obsession with the role of servant. In his superb novel *Jakob von Gunten* (1909), the hero, an aristocrat who has turned his back on his class and enrolled in a school for servants, juggles his urge to become a social "zero" with dreams of grandeur that he cannot entirely suppress.

The blank expression on Walser's face in many of the photographs might almost be that of an inscrutably discreet servant. Where then, we might ask, is the creator of the fictional personae from whose mouths an endless stream of fancies bubbles forth? Walser sheds light on this discrepancy between inner turbulence and exterior blankness in a thinly fictionalized account of his botched audition as an aspiring young actor. The director informs Walser's fictional alter ego that he has no future: "Everything in you is hidden, concealed, deepened, dry and wooden. Inwardly you may be the most glowing person, crumpled, let's say, by passions, but nothing becomes outwardly visible in you."[13] Small wonder, then, that Walser should have decided to drop the stage and take up the pen in earnest—or perhaps, since it is Robert Walser we are talking about, we ought to say, in jest. Walser continues to switch roles in his prose with the dexterity of a writer whose first love was the stage.

In 1905 Walser moved to cosmopolitan Berlin where his brother Karl had established himself as a set designer for Max Reinhardt. Through his brother, Walser came into contact with Wedekind, that enfant terrible of the German stage; von Hofmannsthal; Samuel Fischer, the publisher; and Walther Rathenau, the industrialist who later became foreign minister in the Weimar Republic. Yet Walser never felt at ease in this Berlin world of high culture. He never lost the acute sense of self-irony which ran after him "like a docile little dog."[14] Reverting to his favorite role, he attended a school for servants in Berlin, and subsequently, as Monsieur Robert, polished lamps and waited on table in a castle in Upper Silesia.

In Berlin Walser wrote three novels in quick succession, *The Tanner Siblings* (1907), *The Assistant* (1908), and his masterpiece, *Jakob von Gunten* (1909). Although he received some favorable reviews, Walser was discouraged by the indifference of the reading public and returned to his native Biel in 1913. He reverted there to the neo-Romantic motifs of his earliest prose, without being able to banish dark undercurrents. In "The Walk" (1917), the most characteristic story from the Biel period, his alter ego, an ever-cheerful strolling artist, evades the giant Tomzack, a personification of gloom, and seeks refuge in a fairy-tale-like forest.[15] Walser had written in 1907 in a letter to his editor, the "nonsense" poet Christian Morgenstern, that he would join the army rather than become a "supplier to magazines."[16] That was what he now became, and his short prose appeared regularly in the feuilleton pages of newspapers all over the German-speaking countries.

As long as Walser adhered, superficially at least, to the unwritten rule that feuilleton contributions be amusing and lightweight, editors were happy to publish his stories and essays. But he gradually grew tired of those restrictions and of the "shepherd boyish" style,[17] as he himself later called it, with which he camouflaged his literary sophistication during the Biel years. In 1921 he moved to Bern in a conscious effort to make his writing more international in outlook. But his attempt to shake off the "idealistic burden" of conventional notions of art caused the number of rejection slips to mount steadily.[18] Walser's newspaper audience wanted lighthearted, frivolous "nonsense" from him, not the "nonsense" of the avant-garde.

Walser's keen awareness of his literary roots in non-Germanic soil once led him to assert that he was writing French or Russian rather than German.[19] Walter Arndt's piece suggests that the Russian connection may not be as facetious as it sounds, and France was by no means alien territory to the native of Biel or Bienne, as its French-speaking inhabitants call it.

Walser's "book of myself" is a confession in the tradition of his compatriot Jean-Jacques Rousseau. Walser's sense of flux in man and in nature is close in spirit if not in style to the famous reverie that Rousseau wrote on the island of St. Pierre on Lake Biel before being sent packing by the authorities in Bern: "All is in a continuous flux upon earth. Nothing keeps a constant and fixed form, and our affections which attach themselves to exterior things pass away and change necessarily like them."[20] In Walser's prose the assertions of Rousseau's cadenced rhetoric dissolve into the seductions of rhythm.

Although Walser would have been a fish out of water anywhere, it is tempting to imagine him cavorting with such eccentric and self-deflating spirits as Jarry, Satie, and the *douanier* Rousseau in prewar Paris.[21] Those blithe but self-destructive spirits might have been more congenial company for Walser than the artistic personages of Wilhelminian Germany, in whom the bombast of the detested imperial establishment appears to have left some traces.[22] When Walser was asked in the asylum why he had not gone to Paris rather than return to his native Biel, he replied with an emphatic "Jamais!" After his Berlin debacle, he goes on to explain, he would never have dared show his face in the city where Stendhal, Balzac, Flaubert, and Maupassant had been so productive.[23]

Walser is a quirky one-man avant-garde. Back then, before artistic experimentation had become a marketable commodity, forward-looking artists congregated in smoke-filled cafés with like-minded souls who stood in for the missing audience. Walser, who detested artistic cliques of any kind, preferred his solitary walks. In spite of his fear of fame and success, in spite or perhaps even because of his total isolation, recognition was vital to his survival as an artist.

It may well have been the lack of response to his writing that caused the severe cramps in his hand of which he speaks in a letter to Max Rychner, the editor of the *Neue Schweizer Rundschau*, in 1927. Walser describes the origins of his practice of first writing in pencil in a microscopic script, which he would later transcribe for publication into his copperplate handwriting: "I can assure you that I experienced with the pen a real collapse of my hand (it began already in Berlin), a kind of cramp, out of whose grip I slowly and laboriously freed myself by means of the pencil."[24] This "pencil method" allowed him to overcome his resistance to the act of writing. Later, presumably assuming another role, he would transcribe what are now known as the "microscripts"—the essays, fiction, and poems written in that minute hand. George Avery gives an overview here of some of the material that Walser never transcribed. Two volumes of these microscripts, which have been deciphered at the Robert Walser Archive in Zurich, are due to be published in Germany in 1985.

By the late twenties, apart from occasional drinking bouts, Walser was leading the life of a recluse. He began hearing persecuting voices from which he could find no escape. In January 1929 he was admitted to the asylum at Waldau, the first of the two institutions in which he would spend the rest of his life. Before passing through the main gate, according to his own account he turned and asked his sister: "And are we doing the right thing? Her silence told me enough. What else could I do other than go in?"[25] In Waldau he continued to write sporadically, but, four years later, after his removal against his will to the asylum at Herisau, he fell completely silent. He died of a heart attack at the age of seventy-eight, while out on a solitary walk in the snow on Christmas Day, 1956. Like the Expressionist poet Georg Heym, who foresaw his own death by drowning, Walser seems, in "A Christmas Story" of 1919, to have uncannily anticipated the manner of his own death.[26]

Having exhausted a repertoire of roles in life as well as in prose, Walser appears to have reached almost thankfully for the new role of inmate which he was to play diligently, mending sacks and refusing special concessions, for the remaining twenty-seven years of his life. Walser's literary executor, the writer and critic Carl Seelig, recorded some of his conversations with Walser during the period 1936 to 1956 in *Walks with Robert Walser*, a book that seems more authentic than the often bogus *Conversations with Kafka* by Gustav Janouch.[27] Walser's literary acumen had not diminished, and his often insightful comments on political issues such as the origins of Nazism suggest concerns that are far from parochial.[28] Some of the photographs from those years allow us a glimpse of the wonderstruck dreamer in Walser that he used to take such trouble to hide. When asked once why he had stopped writing, Walser chose to invoke a concern that, as the essay by Winfried Kudszus suggests, is central to his fiction— the ideal of freedom: "The only ground on which a writer can produce is that of freedom."[29]

Upon entering the asylum at Waldau, Walser was diagnosed a schizophrenic on evidence that does not emerge clearly from a cursory seven-sentence report by Dr. Walter Morgenthaler, the psychiatrist who admitted him.[30] There was, of course, a history of mental instability in Walser's family: In addition to the problems of the mother, who was subject to erratic mood swings, one brother died in the Waldau asylum in 1916, while another, a professor of geography at the University of Bern, committed suicide three years later. The family history seems to have preyed on Walser's mind. In his autobiographical novel, *The Tanner Siblings*, the hero Simon overhears a conversation about the hereditary problems of the Tanner family, at which point Simon jumps up and protests against the implication that he too is doomed.[31]

In *The Robber*, a novel that was rediscovered in West Berlin and first published in 1972 as *Der Räuber-Roman*, the split personality implicit in Walser's "pencil method" shapes the ironic and often humorous narrative. The story of the robber, a literary outcast who believes he is being persecuted and who, like Walser, often "steals" his plots from popular novels, is told by a first-person narrator who tries to keep his distance from the hero. Yet the narrative continually drops clues suggesting that the two identities are inextricable. In the last few paragraphs the narrator defends the hero's literary accomplishments, which include collaboration on the present book, and he ends with a plea on behalf of the besieged robber.

The psychiatrist whom the robber visits at the narrator's urging agrees that the hero's role-playing as servant and even chambermaid has preserved his sanity. Serving as his own analyst, the robber links the gratification he derives from his servant fantasies to the sexual sublimation behind his lyrical affair with all of creation.[32] This post-Freudian Francis of Assisi is well aware of the peculiar nature of his libido.

Walser's treatment of his precarious mental state shows a "sovereign attitude" towards that state similar to the attitude detected in van Gogh by the philosopher and psychiatrist Karl Jaspers.[33] Winfried Kudszus suggests that all psychiatric categories, even those less obfuscatory than schizophrenia, fail to do justice to the artist in Walser, and Christopher Middleton sees the sources of Walser's creativity in his distinctive otherness.

What distinguishes Walser's autobiographical project from the traditional motif of the journey to oneself is the "systematic tampering with the self," which Harold Rosenberg sees as characteristic of much avant-garde art.[34] Walser strips the self so radically as to defy the conventional wisdom of psychology. It is the way of mystics and of a few singular artists. In whorls of spiraling irony, which the West German novelist Martin Walser unravels in his essay, Walser's figures sing hymns of praise to whatever demeans and abases them.

Walser's art presupposes the demolition of the self which he describes in the story "Oskar." Oskar, who may have been partly modeled after a schizophrenic Biel eccentric, is one of Walser's numerous self-portraits. He is an ascetic who seeks solace in pleasure rather than in faith. Like certain patients of Freud, Oskar tries to put the pleasure principle out of action. But whereas, according to Freud, psychotic victims of trauma are not consciously aware of the psychic mechanism underlying their avoidance of pleasure,[35] Oskar is clearheaded about his objective. He consciously uses suffering to unclog the sources of pleasure.

Walser is careful to omit from his "book of myself" any chapter about the trauma underlying what Jochen Greven calls Walser's "experiment with the self as man and artist."[36] Perhaps an awareness of that omission dictates Walser's conviction that writing "resides in the manner in which the one doing the writing continually . . . strays around what's at the center."[37] Critics have naturally tried to fill that gap. In his 1929 essay on Walser, Walter Benjamin provocatively asserts that all of Walser's heroes are cured and that the key to the mysterious healing process might lie in *Snowwhite*, one of the Zurich fairy tales included in this volume. It seems unlikely that Benjamin knew that Walser had entered the asylum at Waldau on January 25 of that very year. Subsequent critics have used passages, such as the following from the dramatic sketch *The Boys* (1902), to suggest that Walser's mother plays as crucial a role in Walser's imagination as the father in Kafka's: "All the loving probably has to end someday, but then my life will be at an end . . . since my love of life is nothing more than my love of mother, and she is dead."[38]

I would argue that the emotional force of such passages is deceptive. Unless we want to become victims of Walser's irony, we ought never to forget that his apparent spontaneity is an illusion. Far from being a subjective outpouring, his "confession" is a self-conscious artifact. Walser is constantly lifting the veil and showing us the sleight of hand behind the "partial magic" of the self-conscious tradition.[39] In "Fantasy," the first story in the selection, we encounter the archaic imaginings, the trappings of a romanticized past, only to have the seemingly naïve fantasy self-destruct, or the soap bubble burst, as Robert Musil might say, leaving us with nothing but an empty castle and the final full stop. The parallels between these self-effacing fantasies and the visual arts, which Tamara Evans develops, were not lost on Walser himself, who announces in the title of a prose piece of 1928–29: "Here I am writing decoratively." The undulating surfaces of Walser's canvas and the ethereal fragility of his figures suggest analogies with art nouveau and the Pre-Raphaelites.[40]

In the asylum Walser confessed to a psychiatrist that he had never had an intimate sexual relationship.[41] Scarcely surprising then that critics should often invoke the figure of Narcissus. I would argue that, to be truly useful, the resonance of that invocation has to be extended beyond psychology to the realm of art. Although the mirror of language in which Walser's personae cast their reflections can undoubtedly be traced back to Ovid's pond, his figures are more complex than their classical antecedent in the *Metamorphoses*. They have internalized, in the form of corrosive self-criticism, the doubts about the value of reflections that Ovid's narrator raises: "O fondly foolish boy, why vainly seek to clasp a fleeting image? What you seek is nowhere; if you but turn away, the object of your love will be no more. That which you behold is but the shadow of a reflected form and has no substance of its own." [42]

The "book of myself" charts the fluctuating debate within Walser about the rival claims of art and life. His figures often seem like abandoned orphans, imprisoned in fairy tales that are no substitute for home. If they are artists, they tend to regard their art merely as a depository for emotions that would otherwise have no outlet: "What am I supposed to do with feelings, other than let them wriggle and die like fish in the sand of language?" [43] Far from reveling in this encapsulation of the self, Walser is tormented by the thought that the renewal of pleasure he seeks in his art can never make up for the early loss of life and love.

Walser's self-critical awareness of art as a mere reflection turns his retellings of *Cinderella* and *Snowwhite* into an endless hall of mirrors, a display of self-disillusioned ingenuity that is altogether remarkable in a twenty-one-year-old writer. Although I cannot do justice here to the layers of illusion interwoven with the "reality" of the Grimm brothers' version, I would suggest that Walser's doubts about his art continually disturb the symbolist inwardness of his anti–fairy tales. The two heroines are, of course, none other than Walser himself in drag. So it is hardly surprising that in the eyes of this Cinderella and this Snowwhite no fate could be worse than the happy ending with Prince Charming prescribed by the original tale.

During his years in Berlin, Walser's reflections on the rival claims of art and life take the form of essays and stories about the theater. In one piece for the influential theatrical review *Die Schaubühne*, he calls for a drama of "golden ideal lies." [44] Walser's aesthetic differs from the traditional notion of art as an escapist refuge. Far from distracting attention from the miseries of existence, such golden lies ought to "promote . . . the beautiful, crass disgraces of life."

At the core of that credo is a cult of inwardness comparable only to Rilke's. Yet, in another essay on the theater, a countervoice in Walser proclaims that the artist ought to be first and foremost an exemplary citizen: "In the interest of a healthy communal order we despise talent; unless that is, it were to prefer to become human."[45] Yet, with his characteristic tendency to undermine each undermining, Walser parodies that position in the same essay when he calls for an art that would behave in "as middle class a fashion as a middle class breakfast."

Walser's self-stylizations as an artist reflect the tension between his aesthetic and civic values. In "A Kind of Story" he portrays himself as a craftsman-citizen: "I am a kind of artisan novelist. . . . I tailor, cobble, weld, plane, knock, hammer, or nail together lines the content of which people understand at once."[46] Lurking behind the modernist self-characterization of the writer as a self-conscious craftsman is the Romantic vision of anonymous artisans toiling away selflessly on medieval cathedrals. The alternative Romantic vision of the artist as genius occasionally seduces Walser. Usually, however, as in the real-life role of the servant Caesar and in the story "Genius," he invokes such inflated concepts only to poke fun at himself.

Franz Kafka detected in Robert Walser the "backwardness" of a kindred spirit. In a letter of 1909 to his superior, Director Eisner, at the insurance company (reprinted in part 3), Kafka sees Walser and himself as "people who were somewhat slower at emerging from the last generation than others." At first Kafka pretends to be comparing himself to the hero of Walser's autobiographical novel *The Tanner Siblings* rather than to Walser himself. The fledgling Prague writer of 1909 uses that ploy to concede unobtrusively that Walser and he share the same literary turf. That common turf then becomes the basis for puns about the advantages of being backward.

For obvious biographical reasons, Kafka identifies with the "poor career" of Walser's clerks, but stakes out his own claim when he criticizes Walser's determination to secure the "pleasure of the reader." For Kafka, whose literary judgments are notoriously severe, that is an excessively epicurean objective. Then, however, indulging in wordplay clearly reminiscent of Walser's, he transforms the backward person and writer into a recalcitrant horse on the "running track" (the literal meaning of *Laufbahn*, the German word for career) of a stadium where the orchestra is playing, well why not, *Walzer*—*waltzes* or *Walser* with a *z*. The backwardness of writers such as Walser and himself or, sticking to Kafka's image, the horse's balking at the jump, allows them to convey a fresh and unconventional "total view" of stadium and world.[47]

There is, however, a peculiarly Swiss dimension to the "archaic" qualities in Walser. Swiss writers felt justified in advocating—and occasionally even preaching—civic virtues long after such notions had become objects of derision elsewhere in Europe. There was of course no absolute monarchy to be overthrown, and political and social agitation in nineteenth-century Switzerland pitted the peasantry against the townsfolk rather than the middle class against the aristocracy.[48] Elsewhere in Europe it was the failed revolutions of 1848 that sent artists scurrying toward the sanctum of "l'art pour l'art."

Walser's grandfather, Johann Ulrich Walser (1798–1866), a free-spirited preacher and author of political pamphlets and utopian sketches, played a significant role in the Swiss turmoil of the 1830s. Although Robert Walser's overt political involvement seems limited to a brief flirtation with Socialism during his Zurich years, the legacy of his grandfather can occasionally be detected. As his biographer Robert Mächler points out, Walser seems to echo the spirited individualism of his grandfather in "A Strange City" (1905), the utopian sketch included in this selection.[49]

In a review of books by Walser and Kafka in 1914, Robert Musil charges that Walser "sins" against the rights of objects to be perceived as "real." Shorn of its moralistic overtones, that observation captures in a nutshell the self-doubts that the civic-minded Swiss artist Robert Walser had internalized. In the 1920s Walser's writing becomes increasingly radical as he converts his sin into a full-fledged poetic method. His conception of experience and reality unyokes him from the idealistic burden of conventional genres.

Walser renounces the transitions and "epic connections" that irritate him in favor of an art that relies on juxtapositions rather than transitions.[50] William James might be describing Walser's writings when he observes in "The World of Pure Experience" that "experience itself, taken at large, can grow by its edges."[51] If James expanded our conception of experience in philosophy, thereby helping to usher in the modernist breakthrough in English writing, Robert Walser accomplishes something similar in literature. Perhaps that is why in Guy Davenport's story "A Field of Snow on a Slope of the Rosenberg," William James pays a courtesy call on Robert Walser in Biel.[52]

Walser's Bern prose may prove to be one of the most exciting rediscoveries in his varied oeuvre, which, as of now, runs to twelve volumes in the German edition. The longest story in the selection, "A Slap in the Face et cetera" gives an impression of Walser's range in the Bern period. Unlike those in the Biel prose, Walser's mental perambulations no longer use the strolling artist as a narrative crutch. Courageously dispensing with nature as the screen for his projections, Walser attempts to recreate on the page the associations of a mind in flux. In Switzerland and Germany, it was not until the 1970s that Walser's late prose began to attract sustained critical attention, perhaps partly because experimentation in the stream of consciousness mode never had the pervasive impact on German writing that Joyce assured it in English.[53] However, Swiss writers such as E. Y. Meyer and Adolf Muschg rally around Robert Walser, whose life and work they regard as a model of resistance to the stolid values of middle-class Switzerland.

Cast in the form of diary jottings, "A Slap" pelts the reader with fragments of stories, aphorisms, fairy tales, parables, and parodies. Blithely ignoring the distinctions that enable the rational mind to map out time and space, Walser plays "on the instrument of his fancies" like "a musician on the piano,"[54] as he describes his writing elsewhere in *The Rose* (1925), the collection in which the piece originally appeared.

Throughout the piece carefully crafted stories alternate with seemingly aimless diarylike improvisations. The deliberately incomplete stories are masks that reveal as much as they disguise. Walser's figures have a weakness for platonic relationships that would allow them to indulge their fantasies without fear of losing them to a paltry reality. "A Slap" is no exception. Most telling of all is the final story with the banner headline, THE MAN WITH THE BEAUTIFUL WIFE, in which Walser develops the motif of the romantic triangle towards an ingenious anticlimax. Like his robber, Walser draws parodistically on the plots of popular romances, raising stock expectations that he then abruptly refuses to satisfy, drifting off instead into yet another fragmentary story.

Even at its most burlesque and evasive, the humor of the numerous comic episodes allows for sudden flashes of insight. In the story about the Whisperers and the Boomers, which sets up an opposition between two types—the boorishly loudmouthed and the sensitively reticent—Walser is both absurd and uncannily accurate psychologically. Then, underneath the madcap frolics of a hilarious mountain-climbing episode, which brings Charlie Chaplin to mind, is a parable about an outsider's hopeless jousts with established culture. Walser's sense of hopelessness about his own writing emerges most clearly when he evokes Hölderlin and, between the lines, ponders his own fate. Yet we would do well to be on our guard against easy pathos. After all, even at Herisau, Walser had enough ironic detachment to be able to poke fun at the insistence of "professors of literature" that Hölderlin was unhappy during his last years in confinement.[55]

The words flowing from Walser's pen continually swerve his prose in new and unexpected directions. His sentences always create their own reflective backwash, even when the sentiments seem trite. For instance, when the narrator of "A Slap" says he will leave New Year themes to others, we might assume that he wishes to let other writers handle such seasonal topics. But no sooner is the phrase on the page than it has acquired a different meaning. He now extracts from his phrasing, in a style pursued to a radical extreme in "Cigarette," the admonition that he must do without such seasonal joys so as to be able to record them—the writer's lot.

The hidden agenda of submerged thoughts and desires, first noted by Benjamin, occasionally surfaces in delightful wordplay, which I could only partly capture in the English version. When the narrator speaks of a sleepiness descending on his "tangled being," the German *Wesen* (being) needs only to exchange one consonant to become *Besen* (broom), the very next word: "A broom is what I ought to have taken, to sweep myself forward." But this is not just a play on words. Welling to the surface of the prose is Walser's nagging feeling that he ought to take charge of his personality, ought to sweep all idle fancies from his writing.

In "My Efforts," a retrospective survey of his career, written a year or so before he entered the asylum at Waldau, doubts about the legitimacy of his writing besiege him.[56] Since one side of him is skeptical about the claims of art, he asks himself the question posed so often by irritated readers: "Is it still art, what you're up to?" Later, in the asylum, Walser observes that if he were able to begin all over again, he would write in a less subjective style.[57] Fortunately for us, but perhaps not for him, he had not tried earlier to sweep himself clean in that manner.

The narrator of "My Efforts" responds to the nagging question by first unmasking the idealistic assumption that art can be set apart from life. The uncompromising artist in Walser, who foresaw his rediscovery by a future generation of readers, then speaks over the heads of the uncomprehending public of the day, addressing us, as it were: "If I occasionally authored [*schriftstellerte*] on and on spontaneously, that may have seemed a little comical to the deeply serious minded; but I experimented in the field of language in the hope that there might be in language some unknown liveliness which it would be a joy to awaken." [58]

Both the charm and challenge of that hidden life lie in the relentless weaving process through which Walser's prose sustains itself. Walser does not conceal the transitions merely out of mischief: he assumes that our minds are mobile enough to detect them unaided, as we do in life. Here again William James unwittingly puts his finger on the literary objective of Robert Walser: "Life is in the transitions as much as in the terms connected: often, indeed, it seems to be there more emphatically, as if our spurts and sallies forward were the real firing-line of the battle." [59] This seems to correspond in literary terms to the formalist dictum that the how must inevitably submerge the what. Were it not, that is, for Robert Walser—the Walser who not only welcomes us into the hall of mirrors of his art, but sends us back into life with renewed faith in the connective power of our senses.

# I / Selected Prose

# From Fantasy

We are supposed to write something from fantasy. My fantasy loves all that is colorful and fairytaleish. I have no wish to dream of duties and tasks. Everything nearby belongs to the intellect; everything far away to dreams.—On the lake, whose waves meet the most remote houses of our town, a noble lady and a noble boy are moving along in a small skiff. The lady is most richly and sumptuously dressed, the boy more modestly. He is her page. He rows, and then lifts the oars aloft, letting the drops of water drip like pearls into the great stretch of water. It is calm, wonderfully calm. The wide lake lies there motionless as a pool of oil. The sky is in the lake, and the lake seems a fluidly deep sky. The lake and the sky are both a softly dreaming blue, one blue. The noble lady and the noble boy are both dreaming. The boy now rows smoothly out a little farther, very quietly and very slowly, as if afraid of getting ahead. It is more a floating than a gliding, more a standing still and a remaining motionless than a gliding. The lady smiles incessantly at the boy. She must indeed be fond of him. The boy is smiling from under all the smiles. It is morning, one of those lakeside mornings kissed by the sun. The latter blazes down on lake, ship, on the two of them, on their happiness, on everything. Everything is happy. Even the colors in the dress of the beautiful lady. Colors certainly have feelings, too. Colors are agreeable and match happiness. The lady hails from the castle which rises up on the right shore of the lake, its towers glistening. She is a countess. It was at her bidding that the child unmoored the small boat and rowed it to where they still are, almost in the middle of the lake. The lady keeps her white hand in the greenish blue water. The water is warm. It *kisses* the proffered hand. It has quite a damp mouth for kissing. The white walls of the scattered villas shimmer from the shore. The brown vine hills cast their reflections in the water, the villas do so, beautifully, too. Naturally! Each one has to cast its reflection. Neither has precedence. All forms and colors quickened by the shore are subordinate to the lake, which does with them what it will. It chooses to reflect them. It is the magician, the master, the fairy tale, the picture.—The skiff moves by on this deep, fluid, and undulating picture. It is always the same peaceful passing by. We have already described it, however inadequately said. We? Oh, am I speaking in the plural? That is a writer's habit. When writing compositions, I always feel like a writer. But lake, skiff, waves, lady, boy, and oars may not yet vanish. I wish to glance at them once again. The lady is beautiful and lovely. I know of no lady who isn't beautiful and lovely. But the one in question has such an enchantingly sweet setting, illumined by sun and color, that she is especially so. Besides, she is after all a countess from times long vanished. The boy, too, is a figure from earlier centuries. There are pages no more. Our age no longer has any need of them. The lake, however, is still the same. The same hazy distances and colors of yore shine over it even *now*, the same sun. The castle still stands, but empty.

(1902)  Trans. M.H.


# A Strange City

Once upon a time, there was a city. The people in it were merely dolls. But they could speak and walk, were capable of feeling and motion, and were very polite. They not only said, "Good morning," or, "Good night," they also meant it, quite heartfeltly. These people did have hearts. Besides, they were perfect city dwellers. Somewhat reluctantly, they had softly shaken off all peasant and coarse ways. The cut of their clothes as well as of their behavior was of the finest one could possibly imagine, if one happens, that is, to be a good judge of people or a professional tailor. Nobody was dressed in clothes that were worn out or flapping loosely around the body. Taste had permeated everyone, there was no so-called rabble, all were completely equal in manners and education, without at all resembling one another, which would, in turn, have been boring. Thus, only beautiful and elegant people of free and noble bearing were to be seen in the streets. They knew how to handle freedom with the greatest of finesse, how to direct, restrain, and conserve it. As a result, there were no transgressions of public decency. There were just as few offenses against good manners. The women in particular were splendid. Their clothes were both delightful and practical, beautiful and tempting, as well as decent and charming. Propriety was enticing! In the evenings the young men would stroll along behind this enticement, slowly, as if dreaming, and without lapsing into hasty, lust-filled movements. The women went about in a kind of trousers, a mostly white or light-blue lace trousers, which narrowed into a tight waist. The shoes were colorful and tall, and made of the finest leather. Enchanting, the way each shoe gently molded itself to the foot and then to the leg, and the way the leg felt itself surrounded by something precious, and the way the men felt what the leg was feeling! The good thing about this wearing of trousers was that women put mind and language into their gait, which, when hidden under a skirt, feels itself less subject to observations and assessments. Indeed, there was feeling in absolutely everything. Business went magnificently since people were lively, active, and goodly. Their goodliness stemmed from cultivation and tact. Nobody wished to dispute anyone else's claim to a light and beautiful existence. There was money enough available, and for all enough, since all were reasonable enough to take care of necessities first, and since everybody made it easy for everybody else to make beautiful money. They had neither Sundays, nor a religion whose dogmas they might have quarreled about. The amusement centers were the churches in which they gathered for devotion. Pleasure was for these people a deep and sacred matter. It was self-evident that they remained pure in pleasure since everyone felt the need to do so. There were no poets. Poets would have had nothing uplifting or new to say to such people. There were no professional artists at all since skill-fulness in all manner of arts was so widespread. How good when people have no need of artists in order to be alive to the arts and gifted! These people were that way because they had learned to preserve and utilize the senses as something precious. They had no need to go looking in books for turns of phrase since they themselves had fine, mobile, alert, and quivering sensibilities. They spoke beautifully, whenever they had occasion to speak; they had a mastery of language without knowing how they had arrived at it. The men were beautiful. Their bearing reflected their culture. There was much to delight in and occupy oneself with, but all of it had a bearing on the love of beautiful women. All was linked in a fine and dreamy relation. These people spoke and thought about everything with feeling. They knew how to discuss business matters more sensitively, nobly, and simply than is the case today. There were no so-called higher things. Even to conceive of such a thing would have been intolerable for these people, who saw beauty in everything that existed. Everything that happened, happened vivaciously. Is that so? Really? What a stupid fellow I am! No, there's nothing doing with this city and these people. It is not real. It is nothing but thin air. Away with you, young fellow!

Then the young fellow went for a walk, and sat down on a park bench. It was midday. The sun was shining through the trees, making spots on the path, on the faces of the strolling people, on the hats of the ladies, on the lawn; all was roguish. The sparrows were hopping around lightly, and nannies were rolling little perambulators along. It was like a dream, like a mere game, like a picture. The lad leaned his head on his elbow and became absorbed in the picture. Suddenly he stood up and went away. Well, that's his business. Then the rain came along and blurred the picture.

(1905)   Trans. M.H.

# A Genius

At present I am getting ready to become an actor. By now it's only the usual matter of time before my first appearance on the boards. I am learning parts by heart at the moment. Regardless of this most splendid weather, I spend the whole day seated or standing upright in my lodgings, declaiming in every tone of voice. I am entirely consumed by the demon of the theater, and my shouting has the neighborhood close to despair. What's to become of me? But that's the way it had to be. I hold the miming profession to be the highest and purest of human endeavors and do not believe I am mistaken in this. For the time being I will immerse myself in heroic material; it remains to be seen whether I am the right one to jump into character parts. As for my nature, I am one of the sweetest fellows in Europe, my lips are sugar factories, and my behavior is absolutely chocolate. But then, there is also within and around me a sort of masculine tonality, which is genuinely rocklike. Whenever I think it appropriate, I can turn all of a sudden into stone or wood, and that will necessarily be to the benefit of the lovers I play. People will be shocked by my posture, which is very stale, my eyes will fascinate them, my behavior will daze them, consisting as it does of nothing but glowing gas mantles. I have a back that is somewhat bent in addition to being slightly hunched. This physical deformity will captivate them since I intend to erase it from memory by presenting my numerous inner perfections most graphically. They will see something hideous yet also beautiful, and beauty will carry the day. My head is mighty big, my lips are as thick as heavy folios, my hands resemble elephants' feet, and, what's more, I possess a voice that lends itself to awesome modulation. If that melancholic prince could say he spoke daggers, then I may insist, quite legitimately, that I am speaking and chatting swords. As a boy, I once appeared with the dramatic group Edelweiss, in the role of a house servant, that is. I played badly, for I felt the call to higher things. By now, of course, as far as I'm concerned the matter is resolved. My debut is to take place next week, the play is called *You'll Laugh Yourself to Pieces*. It is to be hoped that ticket-buying ladies and gentlemen will turn up in large numbers; if not, well then, so be it. The apathy of an unappreciative public will never do me in.

(1907)   Trans. M.H.

# Good Day, Giantess!

It's as if a giantess were shaking her curls and sticking a leg out of bed when, prompted by some obligation or other, you go out into the metropolis early in the morning, before the trains have even started running. The streets lie there, cold and white, like outstretched human arms; you go about rubbing your hands together, and observe how people emerge from the gates and doorways of houses, as if an impatient monster were spitting out his warm, glowing saliva. Eyes encountering you as you walk along like this, eyes of girls and of men, some dismal, others joyful; legs passing behind and in front of you, you yourself also legging it, as hard as you can, gazing with your own eyes, with the same looks as everyone else who is looking. Each breast bears some sleepy secret or other, each head is haunted by some melancholy or stimulating thought. Splendid, splendid! So then it's a cold, half-sunny, half-overcast morning, with many, many people still lying in their beds, dreamers who have lived and adventured through the night and half the morning, people of distinction who are accustomed to rising late, lazy dogs who wake up twenty times, yawn and resume snoring, old men and invalids who can no longer get up at all, or only with great difficulty, women who have loved, artists who say to themselves, "getting up early, what rubbish," children of rich, beautiful parents, creatures who are fabulously watched over and protected and who sleep in their own chambers behind snow-white window drapes, their little mouths open,

dreaming as in fairy tales, until as late as nine, ten, or eleven
o'clock. Whatever it is that itches and antsies about at such an
early morning hour in the wildly intertwined streets, if not
house painters, then perhaps paperhangers, clerks who copy
addresses, secretive little agents, also people who want to
catch an early train to Vienna, Munich, Paris, or Hamburg,
usually little people, girls from every possible line of business, wage earners in other words. A person observing the
commotion necessarily finds it unique. So he walks on, and
almost thinks he, too, ought to be running, panting, and
swinging his arms to and fro; the bustle and activity are infectious after all, as perhaps only a lovely smile can be infectious.
No, not like that. There is still something more to the early
morning. It catapults maybe yet another pair of grimly clothed
figures of the night with disgustingly red-colored faces onto
the dazzling powdery white street, where they imbecilically
remain for a good while, holding their crooked sticks over
their shoulder, so as to pester the passersby. How the drunken
night dazzles forth from their soiled eyes! Onwards, onwards.
That blue-eyed marvel, the early morning, doesn't waste time
on drunkards. It has a thousand glistening threads with which
to pull you forward, it pushes you from behind, and entices
and smiles at you from the front; you look upwards to see a
whitish overcast sky letting through a few torn pieces of blue,
glance back behind you to see a person who interests you and
to your side at a rich portal, behind which a princely palace
towers up, sullen and elegant. Statues beckon you from gar-
dens and public parks; you walk onwards with fleeting glances
for everything, for everything in motion and at rest, for
hackney cabs, which rumble along indolently, for the electric
tram, which is now beginning to run and from out of which
people's eyes look down at you, for the idiotic helmet of a
constable, for a person with ragged shoes and trousers, for a
man undoubtedly of once comfortable circumstances who
sweeps the street in a fur coat and top hat, for all things, just
as you yourself are for all things a fleeting sight. This is the
wonder of the city, the way everyone's bearing and behavior
gets lost amid these thousands of types, the way observations

become fleeting, judgments quick, and forgetfulness a matter of course. Gone by. What is gone by? A facade from the imperial era? Where? Back there? Might it be possible for somebody to decide to turn around again, so as to bestow an extra glance on the old architecture? Certainly not! Onwards, onwards. The breast is swelling, the giantess of the metropolis has just pulled on her glittering, sun-filled chemise, with the most sumptuous leisure. Well, a giantess like this just dresses a bit slowly, but, by way of compensation, each of her motions, so beautiful and large, pounds and peals, gives off scent and steam. Hackney cabs with American luggage on top rattle past, mangling the language; you are now strolling in the park; the motionless canals are still covered in gray ice, the meadows chill you, the quivering-frozen appearance of the trees, slender, thin, and bare, drives you on at once; carts are being pushed, two lordly carriages from the coach house of some person with an official capacity rush past, each bearing two coachmen and a lackey; there is always something, and whenever one wants to observe that something closely, it has already vanished. To be sure, you have no end of thoughts in your head during your one-hour march, you are a poet, and besides can keep your hands safely in the pockets of your, let us hope, respectable overcoat, you are a painter, and, in the course of your morning walk, have perhaps already polished off five pictures. You have been an aristocrat, a hero, a lion tamer, a socialist, an explorer of Africa, a dancer, a gymnast or a tavern keeper, and just now have fleetingly dreamt of being introduced to the Kaiser. He climbed down from the throne and drew you into an intimate, half-hour conversation in which the Frau Kaiserin might also have taken part. In your mind, you rode the metropolitan railway, tore the laurel wreath from Dernburg's brow, got married, and made yourself at home in a village in Switzerland, produced a stage-worthy drama—jolly, jolly, more, hey you there, what? What's that? Yes, that's when your colleague Kitsch encountered you, and then the two of you went home together and drank chocolate.

(1907)   Trans. T.W. and S.B.

# Ovation

Imagine, dear reader, the beauty and magic of the moment when, through her abilities and their effect, an actress, singer, or dancer has transported an entire audience to such a pitch of jubilation that all hands are set in motion and the most handsome applause roars through the house. Imagine that you get carried away and that you too pay homage to the brilliant achievement. From the darkened, tightly packed balcony, demonstrations of approval drum down like hailstones, and like drizzle flowers rain down over people's heads onto the stage, some of which the artiste picks up and presses to her lips with a happy smile. Delighted, and lifted aloft by the applause as by a cloud, the artiste throws kisses and a gesture of thanks to the audience, as if it were a little dear, a good child; and the big and yet little child is delighted with this sweet gesture, as, of course, only children can be delighted, time and time again. The rustling soon breaks out into a frenzy, which subsides somewhat, only to break out immediately all over again. Imagine the golden, if not diamond, spirit of jubilation filling the room like a visibly divine puff of mist. Wreaths are thrown, bouquets; and there may be a fanciful baron present, standing right at the edge of the stage, holding his fancy-filled head at the precious little feet of the artiste. And perhaps this aristocratic enthusiast now places a thousand-mark bill underneath the ensnaring little foot of the adored and adulated child. "Keep your riches to yourself, you pinhead, you!" Uttering words such as these, the girl bends down, takes the bill, and throws it back with a contemptuous smile to the donor, who is almost crushed by shame. Imagine this very vividly and more besides, dear reader, such as the sounds of the orchestra, and you will have to confess that an ovation is something magnificent. Cheeks glow, eyes shine, hearts tremble, and souls float around the auditorium like a fragrance, in sweet freedom; and the stagehand has to raise and drop the curtain diligently, again and again, and the woman, who has succeeded in taking the entire house by storm, has to step forward again and again. At last silence falls, and the piece can be brought to an end.

(1912)   Trans. M.H.

## Oskar

He began this strange behavior at a very early age by going his own way and finding such evident pleasure in being alone. In later years he recalled very clearly that nobody had made him aware of such things. All by itself the strange need to be alone and apart had appeared, and was there. All alone he drew from within himself the thought that it is beautiful to shut oneself off so as to gain fresh desire and feel renewed longing for being open and for going out harmlessly among men. It was a kind of calculation that he made, a kind of task that he set himself. He had moved into a wretched, half-destroyed house on the Bergstrasse; he lived there in a shabby little room, which was equipped and decorated with a remarkable lack of furnishings. Even though it was winter, he would have no heating. He did not want any comforts. Everything around him had to be rough, inhospitable, and miserable. He wanted to bear and endure some thing, and ordered himself to do so. And that, nobody had told him either. All alone he had the idea that it would be good for him to order himself to bear hardship and malice in a friendly and good-hearted manner. He considered himself to be at a kind of upper-level school. He went to university there, as a weird and wild student. For him it was a question of observing how far he ought risk pushing himself, how daring he might be. Every once in a while, fear entered his room and grazed him with the cold crêpe of despair. But he had taken up the dare to become peculiar, and he had to keep it up, almost against his will. The oddities take whoever has set foot among them, lead him further, pull him away, never again let him go. His days and his nights he spent alone. Two small children lay in the next room, right against the wall. He would often hear them crying pitiably. He lay sleeplessly during entire long dark nights, as if sleep were an enemy, frightened and fleeing from him, and as if wakefulness were a good friend, unable to tear himself away from him. Every day he went on the same walk through the frozen winter meadows and felt as though he were on a day-long hike through unknown and unfamiliar regions. Each day resembled the next. No young person would have been able to find this way of life beautiful. He, however, wanted it thus; he ordered himself to consider this way of life beautiful. Since he wanted to see attractions, he saw them; since he was searching for depth, he found it; since he wanted to get to know misery, it revealed itself to him. He endured all so-called boredom with joy and pride. To him the sameness and the one and only color seemed beautiful, and that single tone was his life. He wanted to have nothing to do with boredom. So for him it did not exist. He governed himself thus. Thus did he live. He kept company with those calm women, the hours, as though with sensuous and physical beings. They came and went, and Oskar, that was his name, never lost patience. To him impatience meant death. Perseverance, into which he freely and voluptuously sank, was his life as a man. Swathing and surrounding him with the sweet fragrance of roses was the thought that he was poor. He belonged to the poor with body and soul, with all his thoughts and feelings and with his whole heart. He loved the hidden paths between the high hedges, and the evenings were his friends. He knew no higher joy than the joy of day and of night.

(1914)   Trans. M.H.

## An Address to a Button

One day, as I was busy mending the buttonhole of a shirt, which a loud sneeze of mine had ripped apart, it suddenly occurred to me, as I kept on sewing as diligently as an experienced seamstress, that I might address to the honest shirt button, that faithful and modest little fellow, the following words of appreciation, which, though mumbled quietly to myself, were probably all the more sincerely intended:

"Dear little button," I said, "how many thanks, what a good testimonial he owes you, he whom you have served so faithfully, diligently and unswervingly, by now, I believe, for several years. Notwithstanding all the forgetfulness and lack of consideration he has shown at your expense, you have never even suggested that once in a while he might offer you a bit of praise.

"This is the time for it, now that I have a clear idea of what you stand for, of what you are worth. You, who, throughout your long and patient service, have never pushed your way forward into an advantageous and pretty spotlight, or into some beautiful, harsh, and extremely eye-catching lighting effects. You, who chose rather to dwell always in the most discrete of discretions, where you could exercise your dear, beautiful virtue to your utmost satisfaction, with a modesty that is moving, enchanting, and utterly beyond praise.

"You delight me with your proven strength, which stems from honesty and fervor and from your ability to dispense with the praise or recognition coveted by anybody who ever accomplishes anything.

"You are smiling, my dear fellow, and, as I unfortunately can't help noticing, you already look somewhat used and worn.

"My dear admirable fellow! You ought to be a model to those whose utter craving for ever more applause has made them ill, who, unless constantly pampered, fanned, and petted by the goodwill and high regard of all, fall prey to a grief, a listlessness, and a peevishness that make them wish to collapse immediately and die.

"You, why you are capable of living in such a way that nobody has the slightest recollection you exist.

"You are happy; for modesty is its own reward, and fidelity feels comfortable within itself.

"Your refusing to make anything of yourself, your being

nothing more than your lifelong occupation or, at least, your seeming that way, your feeling entirely devoted to the peaceful fulfillment of duty, which one can call a splendidly fragrant rose, its beauty probably almost a mystery to itself, its fragrance wafting without the least intention, since that is its fate—

"Your being, as was said, what you are and your being as you are enchants, touches, captivates, and moves me, and makes me think that in this world, which is rich enough in disagreeable apparitions, there are things here and there that make the person who sees them happy, joyous, and serene."

(1915)   Trans. M.H.

# Jesus

Although all these may be only woolly and unkempt figments, wildly entangled fantasies, configurations of the night, and although I have perhaps, or rather probably, never seen this man, this Jesus, with these eyes of mine, have never even caught a glimpse of him, I would nonetheless almost like to believe that I did see him once, and I would prefer not to doubt that he appeared to me in the snow one day, late of a winter evening, after darkness had begun falling. Right there, in a neighborhood on the outskirts, where wide ghostly pale fields reach up to the last few isolated houses, where wilderness grazes habitation, stroking it gently as it were, it was there he encountered me, there that he came towards me, slowly, with long and hushed steps, ever monstrous and incomprehensible. He resembled one from the dead, one who had just climbed out of the tomb, one who had arisen awesomely all of a sudden, and that he must have done, since Jesus, the noble and great friend of mankind, ought after all be long dead, long buried, long since alive no more. But there he was, alive in the ghostly radiance of the extremely cold evening, wondrously large and beautiful. Oh, it would be a shame if these were only imaginings, nothing but raptures! One so wants, so truly wants to believe in certain things; one forces oneself to, and cannot help but do so. The large and piercingly brilliant stars of the winter skies and the chill cutting through my thin clothes, as I stood there, were truly wonderful. I was shivering in my thin suit, that I still remember very clearly, but a good unending hot joy trembled through me, making me live as I had never lived before, nor ever again would. It is spirit that gives us life, and he, whom I saw striding to and fro in the twilight, was a spirit, surely he was, after all, mainly or merely a spirit, nothing but feeling and spirit. A spirit was shuddering and glowing through me, and everything around me began to sing, talk, and resound. It was the stillness and love that were resounding; and, being most acutely conscious of this, I was pleased. There was an inexpressible joyousness, hope, belief, and love within me, and the mysterious one, standing there, hair falling in delightful golden snakes and waves from head to shoulders, was a sight that made me stare. The beautiful blond hair was like a consuming fire inflaming him, and what's more his expression, no, I must confess, that nowhere else in life have I again seen anything so frightfully beautiful. Such things one sees but once in life and then, never again, even if one were to live to be a thousand years.

It is remarkable, by the way, that it occurred to me the very instant I spotted the strange figure that it was Jesus I am seeing right there in front of me. Since then, I have often thought a lot, especially about this, but have never gotten any wiser. To understand something fully can, at times, mean to lose everything again. Uncertainty is often most beautiful, and majestic configurations do not want to nor ought they be entirely seen through and recognized. It is possible to destroy rather than assimilate one's object of enquiry through penetrating research, immersing it, or so I imagine, in night and invisibility, in sum, I wish to call myself happy whenever I store up an intuition for myself, and have no wish to desire to know any more. So Jesus was not dead: That was the splendid thought, and I clung to it. Love stood there right before me in the snow, beckoning with wondrous tenderness, the heavenly shy eyes glowing with a terrible brilliance. I threw my whole being into the apparition. Wild noises of drinking drifted across from an inn nearby; this has remained as unforgettable to me as the grace and supernatural gentleness of the divine appearance. I asked myself what Jesus was up to, out here at the farthest reaches of the city, whether there was really anything for him to do in the world, and which way he would most likely think of making his presence felt. Strange thoughts ran through my head. Then I went into the house, up into my room, lit the lamp, sat down at the table, took the pen, and carefully noted on a piece of paper the face and all thoughts related to it. When I was finished, I went to the window, opened it, it was late already, and looked out into the night, onto which a half-moon was looking down from its heights, and then I saw the stranger still standing in the road. I would have liked to call out something, but I couldn't find an appropriate word, and my voice seemed cut off from me. I closed the window and got into bed. The following morning, when I went downstairs, it seemed to me that I could see traces of the stranger's feet in the snow. He himself was gone.

(1916)   Trans. M.H.

# The Angel

An angel such as this does well to wait until informed he is needed. Sometimes that takes longer than he expects. He simply has to restrain himself, ought not think he is irreplaceable. I would not like to be the one whom I made an angel. I deified him so that he would never again encounter me, would be unalterable as a picture, at which I could look forever according to my needs and desires, drawing courage from the sight. I almost pity him—he, who thought I was curious and would run after him, whereas I have him, so to speak, in my pocket or like a band across my forehead. I go

to him no longer, but his worth surrounds me, and I see myself illumined by his light. Whoever has known how to give,
has also known how to take. Both need to be practiced. He
came about through compassion, yet it can happen that I, the
beseecher, play games with him. He has doubts, is afraid.
At times I have faith, at times not, and this he must endure,
poor dear.

(1925)   Trans. T.W. and S.B.


# A Cigarette

What a strange sketch this is presenting me with. I
shall enclose it forever even if that makes it go moldy. Today
somebody dropped a cigarette on the ground. I saw it fall. Not
that it aroused any sympathy in me. "She-gan-resc" is what
the she-char-ette made me think. I went on thinking: "What
sort might she be?" "Go rescue her," was what then shot
through my mind. Another case, then. There is a lady in distress somewhere, and the cigarette that somebody dropped in
front of me has reminded me of her. Cigarettes are our lifelong
companions, or those of most of us, at least. They are manu-
factured mainly in Turkey. I am thus either in distress, jammed
in, or there exists somewhere a severely criticized beauty towards whom I might have to play the chivalrous and deter-
mined little rescuer and savior. Would I be the right person
for this? A mission such as that would naturally be very honor-
able. I do, indeed, feel at times I have been somewhat crowded
in, driven into a tight spot, but refuse to take this tragically.
One ought to be careful not to take oneself too seriously. In
any case, I enjoy being at a loss, and if a censured lady exists
somewhere, I shall advise her to consider her condition the
prettiest imaginable so that nobody need order himself to
mount a chivalrous rescue. It does take a little suffering to
make beauties truly beautiful. To me this insight is irrefutable,
and, armed with it, I am continually walking courageously

up to the lady seemingly in need of rescue, who would, I believe, be unhappy, were she to allow herself to be saved. If I am the one in a jam, then I somehow treasure everything unfathomable, irretrievable, and lost since in all tragedy there lies to my mind something joyous, or beautiful in other words, something reconciliatory. To be jammed in, smashed to bits, etc., is certainly tragic, I concede, but I have acquired the rather strange notion that the good can be bad, the free unfree, the loveable blameworthy, the just unjust, and the joyous melancholic. In all constraint there is far more salvation than in all salvation mongering, and I should, therefore, like to do without the latter. It is, of course, splendid to come so nobly to the assistance of a beauty. If I were to doubt that, I would be a scoundrel, spending all my free time smoking cigars et cetera. Yet, have not good deeds often turned into bad ones? I believe in my own supposed distress as well as in hers, but, politely, would like to entreat both of us to be patient and well behaved amidst the sea of vexations. To me rescues seem intolerant by nature; I would, by your leave, therefore, like to refrain from them tenderly, and most humbly ask that in future no cigarettes be let drop in front of me. I met her lately, the lady who wants to be lifted up on high by me or, as far as I'm concerned, dragged down to the depths. For I am capable of either. That I admit. She looked more beautiful than ever. Her distress suited her admirably. The little bit of suffering made her face picture perfect. And there was I, supposed to provide her with so-called happy times? I shall never again do so. I feel responsible both for her and for me, and for the time being will leave it at that. I wrote many years ago that life is long for those who have trust, and still stand behind what I said then. Both the lady in dismay and the crestfallen gentleman ought to believe in possibilities and transformations. One night I saw a gentleman throwing away his half-smoked cigarette with a negligence that was frighteningly beautiful. That made a lasting impression on me. Standing there, illuminated by a streetlight, gazing out into the night life, he threw the cigarette away, as if it were an infertile form of belief, as if getting rid of it had brought him some relief. We can travel, and yet remain the same, can dwell in one and the same place, contemplating the same features year after year, and yet, no matter how extreme the uniformity, go through a wealth of experiences. The way he threw it aside as soon as he decided he no longer liked it! The contemptuous gesture invigorated him. New forms of respect do of course germinate from contempt. How that fellow gazing indifferently into the night life interested me! The cigarette of today brought the earlier one to mind. Past and future circle around us, and signs make existence beautiful. Now we know more, now less. There is always someone thinking of me. I shall never let myself be rescued, nor shall I ever rescue anybody.

(1925)  Trans. M.H.

## A Slap in the Face et cetera

I tied ice skates onto a woman teacher, jumped to attention in front of the sergeant reprimanding me. A thriller lay among my service records. A girl to whom I mentioned this thought that was the right place for it. Once again I tasted the new Twann wine, and saw an ingenious play at the municipal theater. It was awfully nice, the tiny auditorium. Looked at a new railway station, stroked the chin of a lady bartender. When feeling cheerful, one likes to act like a man of the world. In the play I was speaking of there was an actress who had nothing to say the whole evening except "Yes, Mamma"; she did so in every conceivable key. That was frightfully amusing. I was in the standing room, right behind a young woman. Since I had a suspicion her husband was in the immediate vicinity, I feigned indifference, remaining stoical and at ease. When the husband approached, he probably thought I was being quite proper. The smoothly delivered work comes from the pen of a person whom society let drop because of some faux pas. A peculiar pleasure, to delight in scenes whose inventor came to such grief! The entertainment that his talent affords you makes you drop into the most profound astonishment at the possibility of human metamorphosis. I'm speaking of Oscar Wilde. I bought myself biscuits, enjoying some myself and handing others out to a group of boys and girls. Even those I had already bitten into found charmingly ready takers. Oh! Carefree youth! Looking at nice faces makes you nice and observing good manners, well-mannered. In refined surroundings, given just a little recognition, you likewise become refined. I rode in floating seats on a merry-go-round. Wonderful, to glide over people way down there! Do not good spirits often well up from bad? I prefer to be neither always in a good nor always in a bad humor. One mood relieves the other. No person on good terms with himself would care to enjoy his existence undeservedly; if things didn't go badly for him now and then, he would feel he were insulting his fellow men. I asked a woman at an advanced hour: "Mind if I take you along?" By way of answer she said: "A slap in the face, that's what you can take!" A car drove up, and she stepped in. When accosted, women have, I think, the right to respond with whatever crosses their minds. Plucky words from pretty lips can only sound delightful.

On another visit to the theater, I was treated so intimately by the lady taking the coats that I felt as though I were her husband. Had I been honest, I would have had to take care of that woman from then on, and I didn't know her at all. Her being put me under an obligation to her. Blazing like a log, I walked down to the stage and examined the feet of the lady beside me. We let slip countless opportunities to set up a liaison and join ourselves with another in a common destiny, sharing merriment and reflection. But I don't wish to reflect, and would rather say I let my eyes glide down into the orchestra, into the boxes. Eyes are unbelievable gymnasts! While I was looking with great interest at the ladies and gentlemen, their hands and feet began to move. Opera glasses, handkerchiefs, programs came into view; fingertips touched hairdos. One woman in particular was looking around with an astonished air, as if she wished to spot the person causing the disruption. But, at that moment, the curtain went up; I and everybody else now turned our attention to the stage.

I was ambling along aimlessly. The aimlessness I forgave myself wholeheartedly since I realized that we have reason to treat ourselves with forbearance. An intangible sleepiness came over my most tangled being. A broom is what I ought to have taken to sweep myself forward. I got stuck in the muck while gaping lovingly at the velvet blue of the sky. This manner of contemplation was most leisurely. I then whispered in an agitated tone into my own ear—or rather earlet: "How difficult it is to be good!" I let myself off easily here, but find that's only right and proper. I consider it my duty to speak of myself with the necessary respect. In the absence of birdsong, I myself sang an aria from an opera and was extremely satisfied with my performance. In an inn, I sat down beside some small children who had an oblong table to themselves and were behaving as if they were worth taking seriously; they were playing cards and vying for the happiest imitation of adults. There were three girls and a boy into whose hand a cat peeked, and then, hopping over the fan of cards, ingratiated herself deftly with me as I consumed cheese. What she desired was quite obvious. So I stuffed her pretty muzzle with morsels which I duly cut into elegant tidbits. Incisively, yet not without a certain nonchalance, I admonished a youth who was cheekily sprinkling a wall, in his free hand a bunch of flowers wrapped in tissue paper. A small girl had a friend hoist her up by her tiny legs so that she could mail a postcard. From the post office, a clerk watched me as I was looking at the little Ludwig Richter pictures. Oh! Eyes, that spot everything that's afoot! No sooner are you an observer than somebody is observing you—not that it does any harm. In bed I play sweet mamma and child, say my prayers properly, and fall asleep like a good little boy. What one doesn't do to create some diversion! I have had the strangest ideas come to mind, and do hope that they will never abandon me. I'm truly happy only when thinking of something nice, and thus giving myself as much, if not more, than if somebody gave me a present. Remaining cheerful is important to me, since I believe I am good for something.

Last night I woke up, switched on the light, and, as a result of I don't know what sequence of impressions, thought of the one whom they crucified one day. Workmen hired for the task nailed his hands and feet to the wood—hands that had touched feverish foreheads in blessing, that had passed through children's locks, feet that had carried him towards those in need of comfort. The thought of the sufferer did not keep me from biting into an orange, a fruit whose splendidly colored juices magically summon the south. When they drove the nails through his flesh, the blood squirted out at those who had taken this deed upon themselves. Whereupon the cross was erected. This way of curing a person of mischief seems like a game; there's something naïve about the nailing of a living body to a piece of wood: "So you're all tacked up there! A pleasing composition! Now you can savor your martyrdom." As a means of punishment, crucifixion borders on the ridiculous. The earliest paintings depict the people at the foot of the cross dispelling their boredom with games and other amusements, but I don't wish to dwell on this. In the case of holiness so great and so terrible, what seems called for is awe. At school, the pastor told us that the sufferings of Jesus on the cross had lasted about nine hours. But why think of that? By the way, what kind of a face would a contemporary of ours make if he were crucified? To be kissed, to be crucified! I'm now going to sneak away into everyday life. Yesterday I read newspapers in a café. There was an article in one of them saying we aren't Christians any longer, but I don't think that's possible. One can be blissful in suffering—although one would rather not be crucified. How he wailed on the cross, this model of distinction, whose every manner and gesture was so well conceived, who carried himself throughout so exquisitely. Having sided with the poorest, he himself was now one of them; there may be justice to this, but I don't like what I'm writing here. Writers ought not consider themselves great because they fawn on the grandiose; they should rather try to be significant in small things. What was I thinking recently on that score? Knowing how to speak beautifully on the humblest subject would be preferable to expressing oneself poorly on an ample pretext.

When I picture my insignificant and idyllic self, a romantically inclined little being, indulging myself again last night sipping wines, and when I then call to mind Lenin, of whom there has been much talk recently, a question presses itself upon me: Was he alive to the joys of nature? His picture tells the tale of a man hardened by experience. Was he a ladies' man? Amiable, obliging? He was the son of a school inspector, a descendant of oppressors, offspring of people who certainly didn't write poetry and so forth, and hardly had a high regard for music. Yesterday I was a bit frivolous again. Was he ever that way? Did he have soul? I'm enjoying this peculiar investigation. But how did he come to mind? I heard an Italian singer yesterday whose song opened my heart to the sky and carefree ways of the south. Then he came to mind, probably just because of the contrast: a conquerer of the masses, an unfeeling one who cut through men like an earthquake, since the discovery of new methods of putting humanity in order was deemed essential. He once lived in an alley where my lackluster self had taken up lodgings in the house of a very kindly woman. Lenin and Christ? Faith and Love were inscribed, so to speak, on the banners of the latter. When I wax poetical about towering personalities, I easily lose my inner certainty, and for that I take credit. Christ's concern was to develop the life of the soul, Lenin's to expand the life of society, to secure equal footing for all in this earthly realm. Which of the two drew from the better spring? I want to speak of something else for I'd consider it a waste of time to continue along these lines. One more thing: there are people who are normal citizens but indisposed artists. An artist can be somehow ill, and yet have stature as an artist. If a healthy person writes badly, then he's a sick artist. If a sick person writes well, then, as an artist, he belongs among the healthy.

Snow covers streets and squares, monuments and roofs, and that's as it should be in the New Year season. I gladly leave Christmas trees and candy to others. Writers are marvelous at observing the joys of their fellow men without immediately thinking they ought to share them. A warm room is already quite a bit in winter. Am I not reading a little book entitled *As True as Gold*? "Good day, Mrs. von Rubberstamp," was how I recently greeted the wife of a manager who goes by another name. She exclaimed loudly, "What's wrong with you?" "I'm in a good mood," I replied. My first evening at the theater was on New Year's Eve, and I carried the exalted impression that it made straight home to my parents' house. On a sky-blue spring day a mother was waiting for her beloved son, Lieutenant von Schoellermark. There was an energetic knocking at the door; who was it but the desired one, and they soon lay in each others' arms. Then he went to Berlin, where he got to know the most fabulous dweller of the Motzstrasse or millionairess; she was young and incredibly beautiful. They met in Tiergarten Park, and sailed together on skates around Rousseau Island, which looked pretty in its December garments. The Beauty told him, as she was accepting kiss after kiss from him, that her father had other plans for her. He staggered back, experiencing his moment of great disillusionment, all of which I have culled from a keepsake album. I'd now like to disclose something about myself. I must confess that, as a child, I negligently wrote *I wih* instead of *I wish* on a list of New Year wishes. The way such things stick in one's head! The young Napoleon was already winning snowball battles as a pupil in the school yard at Brienne. Snowmen have a wide mouth and not very impressive eyes, they hold a broom in one hand, and stand incredibly still. "Between Two Hearts" is the title of a moving story which I have incorporated into my tiny library: A wealthy suitor, no longer young, gives up his sweetheart in favor of a penniless rival whose youth bursts from his countenance. The girl's name was Roberta and the lucky boy's was Max. The following day all three were sitting together peacefully. Conceivable that they sat at table and satisfied their appetites. I overheard a nice young person introducing himself smartly to a landlady as a kitchen boy. Whenever we awaken respect, we generally do so behind our backs; that's why we never find out about it. The people who find us likeable keep quiet, and that's just as well, otherwise we'd take ourselves too seriously. A haberdasher told me courtesy is the best policy, and I agreed. At New Year's we give presents, and receive some in return. Both accepting and giving ought and, indeed, need to be practiced. I remember a faintly colored drawing: a white-feathered angel gazing through a tiny window into a room in which the Christ child lies—only a small drawing, and yet I haven't forgotten it. You can forget a lot and recall a lot. The recovery of a little stray sheep is splendid news in the realm of memory; having found its complement, the loss endears itself.

I have certainly made many mistakes with women, but I have never used in their presence a certain little word that I heard a gentleman utter the other day. The young lady was virtually sagging, was getting noticeably smaller under the load. Under which load? I'll let you know. She was about to beam. Otherwise quite a nice fellow; she, as I said, charmed. He, full of witty tales; she, full of desire to listen to his fizzing. In her eagerness not to miss anything she practically cocked her ears. Just then that word escaped from his mouth. He meant no harm by it; it popped out quite inadvertently. A quiet, restrained torment twitched across her face; I found that amusing. I'm malicious, that's what it is. She would have liked nothing better than to deal her recent idol a blow, but was in no condition to do so. She peered into space as if expecting to snatch composure from some nook or other. Her excitement was delicate and frightening, insignificant yet terrible. He said something very simple, and from the mental summit that yielded the platitude, asked her:

DJAGETME?

As compassionately as if she were his pet beetle, his little leaf, his shrinking violet of a Luise from [Schiller's] *Intrigue and Love* or a deprived little birdbrain. She smiled with great difficulty after a hard-won struggle with herself. He failed even to notice the great exertion which he had caused. And thus the most loving of efforts are often overlooked. Her inner struggle was as worth seeing as his failure to notice it. While observing this, I read a "Woman's Supplement."

What an unpleasant lot, to hang on the wall of a restaurant! To flower on a poster, only to vanish again. Posters and public readings, one after the other! A tender sadness takes hold of me at the thought of all these entrances and fleeting exits. There a gentleman, now a lady. How they must exert themselves, doing so gladly, no doubt! Then along comes the usual respect-inducing article. Yet, something is amiss in all this. How they caper on, latest book in hand only to bow off again! Each act is aware that a new one is about to follow on its heels. Fresh posters always announcing fresh fodder for those being offered the opportunity to spend an edifying evening. Where will it all end? Some writers, the ones in vogue, come frequently, but the supply of poets and poetesses will run out someday. What then? We live in postered up times. The guys with an abundance of ideas in their heads consort with the vulgar. Not a single one has retained a shred of mystique. Outlandishness shrivels from day to day. There seems to be a factory at work, converting the extraordinary into the ordinary. Shy poets are a thing of the past. Will I also make an appearance at the lectern and become profane? Until then I'll go on believing, hard and fast, that I never shall. The noble Hölderlin was destroyed by an excess of love, greatness, and by artistic silence. I'm in such a good mood I'm ashamed of myself. Will I, too, have my poster some day? Will I be overwhelmed by it all? Ought I to steal the show on the wall for a while, only to make way for the next? A postered lady, who had just been tacked up and taken down, was out walking with me. It was a wonderful afternoon; how touching, the way the little branches soared up into the air! "How is it," she asked, "that you can live without laying eyes on any posters of yourself?" I looked at the ground and replied: "I'm afraid for my little bit of happiness."

Yesterday I climbed a mountain. The ascent was going well until I came to sheer ice and couldn't find a foothold. There was not a single tiny tree to be grabbed. So dignified bearing was of no further avail. Then I had an idea, which, by the way, was obvious enough, I got down on my hands and knees and devoted myself for a while to the predictably delightful art of crawling; I believe we have to be capable of adapting ourselves to new situations. There was obstinacy in my crawling, since, after all, the object was to arrive at the top. Had I not bent down, I would have come to a stop. There is pride even in pliancy. The attending difficulties forced me to undergo transformatory measures which were not exactly pretty looking, but what was important to me was covering ground. Did it not look as if I were rejecting "civilization," whereas I was actually trying to preserve it? The smoothness of the ground required a certain smoothness of me, too, and that my character supplied. Pride made me behave without pride, tenacity like a weakling. A voice inside me cried out incessantly, "Get up there!" Can one march up the side of a glass mountain with the dignity of a man of importance? The important thing for me was to reach the top. After all, it's not for nothing that our legs aren't sticks. So why not make use of talents? It pays to be on one's best behavior with mirror-smooth surfaces. Since I couldn't make what was impassible vanish, I embraced it. Don't even the most stubborn occasionally act meek in order to get their way? Whoever kneels can arise again, and it then appears to him that he stands all the more securely. The movement has given him great joy. What fun to scramble or coax one's way up something! Acting like a slowpoke for the sake of speed, well, why not? Trying to get up there is better than being on top; I liked myself better when I was looking up than when I was smugly looking down. Scouting around for a path or a foothold, having to be a bit anxious, the moment of certainty, how exciting that all is!

A Whisperer was sitting quietly all by himself, when there appeared a Boomer, whose loudness the Whisperer saw from afar. One can tell Boomers by their mere looks.

While the Boomer was talking, the Whisperer clung to his whispers. He said to himself: "If I show I'm taken aback, the Boomer will only put on a more earsplitting display."

The voice of the Boomer was pealing like a bell, while bliss blossomed within the Whisperer.

While virtually never ceasing to smirk, Boomers turn into Bruisers, and forget the splendid canons of peace lovers.

Laughter suddenly began to spread all over the Whisperer's face; he found both himself and the Noisemaker comical.

Now when the Pealer saw how pleased the Husher was, deep shadows began crossing his countenance. He had thought that he would erupt, that he'd throw a tantrum.

The Strong at times overrate their strength.

The Clamorer shuddered when he saw his musical offering being laid on the scales to no end. "What a scoundrel!" he thought of the Whisperer.

It is base not to allow oneself to get worked up? Boomers say: "We don't need Whisperers," whereas the latter are again of the opinion that bellowing is superfluous. Who's right, the Thunderers or the Dopey-Heads?

The war between the Shy and the Shameless will probably never, never end.

Boomers are unhappy if they may not boom; as are Whisperers if they cannot abandon themselves to their whisperishness.

The Boomers at first shatter the Whisperers, but a Mute is more astute, and a Shrieker meeker.

How terrible when a Boomer whispers and a Whisperer booms! Such cases are worth seeing.

If a Whisperer fails to begrudge the Boomer's chest-notes, the Bearer of the Idea of Loudness senses this, and becomes unfaithful to his Ideal. And whenever the Boomers find the Whisperers pleasant, the latter start to chatter like sparrows. Consent is but the first step!

Boomers thus see to the booming of Whisperers and Whisperers to the refining of the Unrefined; an unforeseen solution!

In Thuringia, let's say in Eisenach, there lived a so-called bugologist, who, once again, had a niece. When will I ever be done with nieces and so forth? Maybe never; then woe is me! The girl in the house next door was suffering a lot under scholarly tutelage. Wasn't a lieutenant once again fighting in Africa against godless bushmen, who went about wielding spears, clad in nothing but swimming trunks? Then he arrived home, laden with laurel leaves, and lo and behold the girl under entomological tutelage and the victor over the Hottentots found each other! A find that meant a lot to both of them. The caresses amid the shrubs and all the little dove dreams fluttering up from there would require a little chapter in itself. His eminence remained ensconced in his expertise, while all things deep and high, as well as under and above him, and all things circumambient, wafted past, by which we mean knowledge and life, neglecting each other as usual, but that I cannot help.

Not far away, in a castle with a slate roof, which glistened in sunshine, there lived a proud woman who hated her spouse, yet never strayed an inch from his side, conceding him that much since she wished him all the worst. Her name was Lady Firthicket, unless my memory, which is at times faithful, at others forgetful, has abandoned me. The Firthicket had an eight-year-old son. Am I not mistaken? No, not at all! Living in isolation in one of the numerous chambers, the little boy occasionally received visits from his mamma, who intentionally bit the dear lips and furrowed a forehead otherwise so beautiful. Words like *termagant* ought not slip from any pen. An inheritance weighed upon the pitiable shoulders of the youth. To be so ignorant, yet so well endowed. And not even eating adequately. When asked by Lady Hypocrite whether he lacked anything, little trouser-legs could only tremble. I say nothing, either, staying delicate, preferring to stretch a leg in the park, in which, according to Goethe's aphorism, the trees failed to grow to the heavens and where everything looked like a scene by Hans von Marées, all fountains and dragons. I'll let the boy pine away interestingly. Who knows, perhaps he loved his suffering and the one who didn't relieve him of it and who loved him too, so as not to be dear to him? He once wrote her the following: "I am a defenseless match for you, although I don't even get a bib tied around me. Please give the necessary instructions. I wish to admire you constantly."

Now I could pluck at this letter forever, but I'll leave it brief so that people will think about it.

For the girl next door and the young boy as well, I drew on newsstand sources, in other words, on dime novels.

Now engaging my attention is

THE MAN
WITH THE BEAUTIFUL WIFE.

He looks serious, although he has absolutely no right to do so, since he has a beautiful wife, which ought to make him cheerful. I, who lack a beautiful wife, only usurp cheerfulness. The man with a beautiful wife is forever staring at me, as if he wanted to warn me emphatically about beautiful women. When I see him, I say to myself: "Isn't the man approaching the one who, I've been told, has a beautiful wife?" I am not denying that I find him interesting. Who would not be won over by a figure making his entrance linked to an apparition, who, according to my informants, is reputed to be beautiful? Had I a beautiful wife, I'd probably be worried too. But it's well worth giving up a carefree existence for the sake of beauty. When he is looking at me, I behave as though it were or might be so. Whether he thinks I'm interested? He almost has to, and some day he might invite me to his beautiful wife, but most likely he will not. The way we observe each other is truly a dragged-out duet of mutual scrutiny.

Neither he, who has a beautiful wife in whom I believe, nor I, who cannot make anyone believe in a beautiful wife, utters a word. I'm interested in him because I've heard about his wife; he has no interest in me because I don't invite him to meet a wife I don't have. But that which has not yet come to be, might some day come to pass. Just recently, he didn't as much as glance at me, almost as if his beautiful wife had found me wanting, which is impossible, since she doesn't know me. If I were able to meet her and calm down, but what am I saying? In that case he would be the one to lose his calm, and he has enough worries as it is. Beautiful women demand from their husbands an abundance of care. Could I have phrased myself more carefully there? One must deal circumspectly with a man who has a beautiful wife, just as he himself must deal cautiously with someone who has none and might like to get to know one; an opportunity that is better withheld than granted. Were I to see her, his face would probably become even more serious. How could I assume such a responsibility? No, I'll let matters rest at my interest in the beautiful woman with the good husband; for if I bored her, what then? And if I amused her, what then? Let him be content with his wife, who is, one may hope, already a little tired of him. If he were to read that, he'd get ideas into his head. His beautiful wife enchants me since he has not yet invited me to meet her, and I can consider her beautiful, which is advantageous both for him and for me, and for her as well, interested as she is in goodliness, on which note I conclude a series of observations.

(1925)   Trans. M.H.

# Letter to a Commissioner of Novellas

It isn't as though I were too indolent to take under serious advisement the question of pondering your esteemed commission to supply you with suspenseful novellas. In taking the liberty to give due weight to your encouragement, I permit myself to wonder whether I am the proper personage for the manufacture of the article you wish me to supply. After scrutiny of every phase of the issue I have been led to the recognition that I subscribe to the view that, in the first place, I have experienced very little in the course of my life, and accordingly regard, in the second place, my highly respected colleague McCauliflagh better qualified than myself to satisfy your requirements, which are admittedly in some respects not at all totally incomprehensible. To be sure, McCauliflagh, whose temper, as you know, is on the deep-delving side, does not write in a style that is markedly amusing, or suspenseful, or ravishing, or gripping. Perhaps you will be kind enough to give me leave to reveal to you my virtual conviction that cases of talentedness like Maupassant's and Chekhov's, given the civilizational concentration and cultural excultivation that obtain today, have become as rare as can be? Who in our day still lives and loves suspensefully and grippingly? Where does one who carefully keeps eyes and ears open with a view to novella writing and the like encounter any human behavior marked by, or evincing, anything congenial to short fiction? While deferentially requesting you not by any chance to take the raising of such a question in ill part, I do submit that you are broadly, not to say very acutely, aware of the fact that almost all writers now living and creatively active concern themselves by preference with the kind of problematizing that spans all humanity, as it were, and consequently, let us concede, fails to move or grip in other ways. I too have joined the ranks of the belletristic authors who cozily report, personably and circumstantially weigh a great many factors, reach for and scramble up summits of thought and slither down into depths of contemplation, not entirely dissimilar to scholars at their research. I too, like many another who used to create boldly and gaily, have found it increasingly more difficult to be loose, *léger* to put it in French, or in other words not to gaze too far out to a horizon that is always too spacious by comparison. Life in our day gives the appearance of a pleasingly rounded mannerliness, a well-leveled existentiality; a similar semblance prevails in the books that are being written and whose contents deal predominantly with matters of a weighty and summary nature, whereas the novella in my experience tends to occupy itself with what is remarkable about some detail. Where these days do you come across something remarkable, something that stands out in a tangible, visible way from the mass of remaining, not very *telling* visibilities? My colleague Rheutabaguer, with whom I would take pleasure, in principle, to be instrumental in placing you into relations of fruitful augury, is enabled by his ebulliently developed gift of observation to write with uncommon finesse. What is more, he experiences every day some lacy-pantsy adventurette, whereupon he repairs to his studio and, having fastidiously seated himself at his line-turning lathe, produces graceful essays rather than exploiting his experience for a long short story. Just as life, as I have seen it and expect to be able to see it in the future, has as it were turned into something tentative, cautiously groping, so the same thing has happened in recent years to the writing of fiction—which has been and will remain an analogue to life. As life turns finer or subtler, art too becomes more thoughtful and responsible; and a calm reply to your query whether I was capable of being gripping takes on the hue of what was conveyed in it—as I would ask you kindly to take the trouble to note. The novella writer who goes too briskly at the story that is taking shape under his pen, and which is meant to turn out gripping, is apt to make the unedifying discovery that it up and runs away from him, so to speak, i.e., that all grippingness has evaporated. Although I do not set much store by intentions, I intend to hope that I might be prompted to think it would be nice if at some point I were to bring off a novella that would be to your liking; to which I might add that I strive daily to be active, a thing that many a person may claim.

(Late 1920s)   Trans. W. A.

# For Zilch

The piece of prose that apparently wants to come into being here is being written in the dead of night, and I am writing it for Zilch, the Cat, that is to say for everyday use. Zilch is a kind of factory or industrial enterprise, for which writers produce and deliver daily, perhaps even hourly, with steadfast zeal. It is better to deliver than merely to enter upon pointless discussions about delivery or in chatterboxious prattle about service. Here and there even poets will create for Zilch the Cat, telling themselves that they find it more sensible to do something than to refrain. Whoever does something for her, for that quintessence of commercialization, does it for her enigmatic eyes. You know the Cat and you don't; she will slumber and purr with pleasure in her sleep, and looking for an explanation, one is faced with an impenetrable riddle. Although it is recognized that the Cat jeopardizes something like personal development, one seems unable to get on without her, for Zilch is the very time in which we live, that for which we labor, which gives us work to do, the banks, the restaurants, the publishing houses, the schools, the Leviathan of business, the phenomenal range of manufacturing activity, all this (and more if I were to list in numerical order—a thing that just might happen—all I consider redundant) is Zilch, Zilch. Zilch to me is not merely anything that is good for the running of things, that is of any kind of value to the machinery of civilization, but she is rather, as I have said, the whole works themselves. And only such items could possibly aspire to be exempt from Zilchery as can demonstrate so-called eternal values, as for example the masterpieces of art or the deeds that tower high over the hum and drum, the rush and roar of the day. Whatever is not eroded and consumed by favor and distaste—by the Cat in other words, who assuredly is an august entity—may be taken to be lasting and to gain the port of a remote posterity, much like some vessel of freight or state. My colleague Binggeli in my opinion writes for Zilch in every respect, even though his prose and verse are extremely demanding. Regarding the Zilchitude of his otherwise doubtless excellent literary output, Dinggelari (who calls a ravishingly beautiful woman his conjugal own, who dines and sups famously, takes splendid promenades every day, inhabits a flat in a romantic setting) is a prey to egregious error in that he persists in thinking that the Cat will have nothing to do with him. While she considers him her own, he strains to think that he is unsuitable in her eyes; which by no means squares with the facts.

The Cat Zilch is my name for the contemporary world; for the afterworld I do not presume to have a colloquial term.

The Cat is frequently misunderstood, people turn their noses up at her, and when they give her something, they do so with a quite inappropriate attitude—remarking arrogantly "it's for Zilch," as if all human beings had not busied themselves for her from time immemorial.

All that is achieved goes to her first; she eats with relish, and only what lives on and works despite her is immortal.

(1928–29)   Trans. W. A.


# A Sketch

I tremble less at the whims and oddities of others than at my own which lead me to a house, whose appearance I know not whether to describe or leave undepicted.

Just as much as at the house, I tremble at the garden, in which lies undiscussed the house which I am leaving formless, since this may perhaps even be beautiful.

Light trembles in the garden, restfulness rests, and it is no doubt conceivable that a simpleton of a page is simple inasmuch as he leans dreamily against the house and is a small woman in disguise.

The interior chambers of the house are animated by a woman who is real. The people of the house, in which nobody has ever done any cooking, live from love.

It occurs to me to say a happy man arrived just then from afar. He seems to have been a person who believed he had occasion to take constant delight in his delightedness, which he much loved. Fortune was playing with him, and he felt fortunate mainly for that reason.

When the extremely dashing chap looked up at the house before which he chose to stand, he beheld a figure gaping contentedly down at his arriviste manners.

The movingly beautiful and deft one said in a pleasant enough manner: "I was young, and did not know it, considered myself old, and was never convinced of this, and the gratefulness within me proved utterly ungrateful."

"That's the way you look," replied the other.

"Who are you who look at me with almost eerie ease?"

The one looking out the window possessed sufficient high spirits to respond: "I am life. I look down at you from above. You are the lovable conception of life, which by now allows you to live almost too gracefully. Your gazing interestedly up past me is a pleasure that, I believe, I may be able to grant you."

The page's costume makes the page seem like any young person; the woman in the house, inasmuch as she knows she has admirers, lacks something.

The garden somewhat resembled a thought fortunately not thought to a conclusion, and, without having any idea where I get the effrontery to do so, I compare my sketch with a swan singing with unheard of ardor and screechingly giving voice to unmediated things.

(1928–29)   Trans. M.H.

# 2 / Three Poems, Some Forethoughts, and Two Fairy-Tale Plays

# A Little Landscape

A little tree stands in the meadow
and many more nice little trees besides.
A little leaf freezes in the frosty wind
and many more lonely little leaves besides.
A little pile of snow glimmers by the brook
and many more white little piles besides.
A little hilltop laughs down on the valley
and many more nasty hilltops besides.
And behind all this the devil
and many more poor devils besides.
A little angel turns aside his weeping face
and all the angels of heaven besides.

(1898)   Trans. M.H.


# And Went

He waved his hat gently
and went, they say of the wanderer.
It tore the leaves from the tree
and went, they say of rough autumn.
She handed out favors with a smile
and went, they say of her majesty.
It knocked every night at the door
and went, they say of grief.
He pointed tearfully to his heart
and went, they say of the poor man.

(1899)   Trans. M.H.

# Poem from the Microscripts

In the hamper or laundry basket
standing in my bedchamber
the sound of coughing at night
as if somebody were lying there
and as if sitting on the basket
a *whispering* slave, my cruel
servant, my firm resolve
to belong to myself. My thought
*it knows* me. How often is frightening to me
what I think, and I climb out
of the night as out of a granite tomb
and out of haunted sleep as out of
a past of many poor tormented souls
flinging pale images around their temples
and can in the morning again find joy in my life.
Upon nobody would I wish that he were I.
Only I am capable of enduring myself:
To know so much and to have seen so much
and to say so little, so little.

(1924–25)  Trans. M.H.

*Passages that were difficult to decipher are given in italir

Walter Arndt

# Forethoughts to Walser's Fairy Plays

One of the better words for Walser's cast of mind is *tiefsinnig*, a useful semantic blend of "profound," "self-absorbed," and "having either less or more than the standard quantity of marbles." He can be puckishly portentous, ominously playful, cryptic in a way to provoke nervous laughter on a rising note. Reading one's way into Walser as an outsider has, it is safe to generalize, four typical stages: BEFORE, BEFOGGED, BEMUSED, BESOTTED; this merely by-standing translator (a *Beistand* to the reader only linguistically) is at best between the second and third stages. Though by-standing, spiritually he is seated at the feet of those razor-keen, Kafka-casqued, *Kleistbegeisterte* or *-verkleisterte*: the now tweed-, now straitjacketed initiates of the Walser cult.

We have certainly been in unusual company in these fairy plays, most readers will agree; though the first performance in English of *Cinderella* at Dartmouth College in 1983 showed that the plays will take on a compelling life and comic verve of their own in a severely stylized, almost disembodied stage setting. In *Cinderella* we have a king who is a rumbling, fumbling, fumingly good-natured bear, but has not really any place in the play (save as *komischer Alter*), either in the original or in the present one. Then we have a princeling who wavers between being a young Malvolio, embroiled with a Shakespearian fool, and a sappy Hamlet who soliloquizes while hunting on horseback. Not a great prize, surely, this princecompoop, for an emotionally sophisticated if necessarily devious girl like Cindy, except for the fact that she shows a strong streak of masochism and by long practice has made herself impregnable to insult and suffering. For that matter, even this addled suitor is preferable to life at the feet of the two suitably spiteful and pickle-faced sisters, and not just because he has a key to the kingdom's executive washroom and probably to the vault as well. Rather, the attraction of the prospect is that if he should turn out a bully, she could joyfully turn the other cheek as practiced with the sisters; if, as is far more likely, he would turn out malleable, she would have the unwonted chance to mall him to her heart's content and, perhaps, make a full-size and worthy prince of him.

Is Cinderella an ingénue or a Medea in the making? Is her entry into a dual and public life, from an obscure and desolate existence in freedom of mind and soul, a difficult sacrifice to her, as the final scene suggests? Walser readers I know have seldom resisted the temptation to derive, or contrive, conventional (if encoded) sense from Walser's fairy plays. They have done this by literary sleuthing via Kafka and Morgenstern or by American sychahlogy (either depth or shallow); but the attempt is fraught with the risk of unwittingly playing into Walser's hands. He is not your ordinary honest psychopath but an insidiously wide-eyed mild-and-mellow one. One senses too acutely that he thinks of the reader as *his* meat, not the other way round. And if you take refuge in the comforting assumption of at least intermittent dementia on his part, you are likely to see him, in his own good time, turn around, fix you with those seductively long-lashed eyes, and flute: "Ah, imbécile lecteur, mon semblable, mon frère."

Again, then, what to make of Cinderella in this dreamy play? She, like her spiritual sister, Snowwhite, in the other play, seems a kind of wronged but resilient Ophelia. She will get along quite nicely, thank you very much, with or without the bantam-weight Prince whom the fairy tale (or personified, Fairytale) in its dubious wisdom but unquestionable authority, has in store for her. Cinderella is the kind of girl, however, (bad word that, *kind*, she hardly fits any category) who may suddenly drown herself, singing a merry ditty that will break your heart; or when another mood prevails, may lovingly disembowel one of her sisters, persuading us that this is best for both parties. The word for her is *fey*, perhaps. Cinderella also has, it seems to me, the quality of one of those pensively striding Pre-Raphaelite (later, art nouveau) maidens, holding a lily in her hand, with her luminous gaze upon it, and hardly able to *walk* with all that brittle chastity and that subtle whiff of decadence that wafts from her. One may think of Dante Gabriel Rossetti and of Arthur Rackham (both contemporaries of Walser); also of the Rilke of the *Stundenbuch*, three years Walser's senior; and finally of one ten years his junior—arguably the finest, certainly the feyest, of the four greatest Russian poets of this century—Anna Akhmatova.

Now let us consider the following corpus, which is, obviously, not drawn from *Cinderella* or *Snowwhite* but mostly from Walser's quasi-autobiographical prose. It may set Walser against an unexpected foil in a way that may prove instructive:

I am a wicked person, in other words, a person of breeding and education. Persons of breeding have the right to be wicked. Only the lower classes feel it their duty to be virtuous. What was it that I inflicted upon a clerk in an office? I did not agree that he was right in every way, and his anger made him sick. Things went downhill with him as a result, while I managed to stay on top.

I am a sick man. . . . I am a hostile person. Yes, I am not a pleasant person at all. I believe there is something wrong with my liver. I don't know the first thing about my liver, nor whether there is anything really wrong with me. I am not under medical treatment nor ever have been, though I do respect medicine and doctors. In addition, I am extremely superstitious, at least sufficiently so to have a respect for medicine. I am well educated enough not to be superstitious, but I am superstitious anyway.

A pretty young girl wanted to know whether I was an admirer of hers. Since I failed to display any understanding, things went downhill with her, while I managed to stay on top. I don't suppose you will understand that; well, I do. For a while I loved a girl because she definitely seemed a bit dim witted. Imbecility does have a certain fascination.

About my disorder, the truth is that I refuse medical treatment out of rancor. I don't suppose I shall be able to explain who it is I am actually trying to goad in this case by my hostility. I realize perfectly well that I can't "get back at" the doctors by refusing to be treated by them.

I bow to the ladies, only to cut them the next day, thus spreading discomfort. Other people's discomfort comforts me. How fatuous cheerful faces are; how comic serious ones! Whenever people used to come to my office on some business, I snarled at them and felt as pleased as punch when I succeeded in making one of them really unhappy. They were mostly a timid lot; what else can you expect people who come to a government office to be? And what was the main point about my malevolence? Well, the whole point of it, I mean the whole nasty disgusting part of it was that all the time, even at the moments of my greatest exasperation, I was shamefacedly conscious that I wasn't at all a hostile or even an exasperated person, but was merely frightening sparrows for no reason in the world and being vastly entertained by the pastime. I might be foaming at the mouth, but just present me with some little toy, give me a nice cup with sugar added, and I shouldn't be at all surprised if I calmed down completely, were deeply touched, even. . . .

I am a person who does not know precisely who he really is. Sometimes I am as sensitive as a girl.

What a bore it is to hear people talk about the countryside and all that! People of education should realize that it is tawdry to resort to the exclamation "wonderful!" when discussing a work of art. Praise can strike one as pretty idiotic. Being in raptures verges on stupidity at times. Happy people easily make themselves unpopular. Isn't it almost shameless to flaunt one's high spirits, to let one's eyes shine so freely? Any minute the elation may fade away. We ought to ration our contentment. . . .

Incidentally, I was rather exaggerating a while ago when I said that I was an ill-natured official, for actually I never could become a spiteful person. I was always conscious of countless elements in myself that were absolutely contrary to that. All my life I felt them simply swarming in me, asking to be released, but I wouldn't let them. I deliberately wouldn't let them. . . . Not only did I not become hateful, I didn't even know how to become anything, hateful or good, a villain or a decent person, a hero or a worm. I prefer to be accommodating when no one expects it rather than when people think I am doing so gladly. Nobody is entitled to treat me as if he knew me. When I recognize somebody, I don't betray it to his face; thus appearing crass and arousing displeasure. . . . I console myself with the rather ill-natured though entirely useless thought that an intelligent person cannot become anything in particular, and that only a fool succeeds in becoming anything. Yes, a man of this century must be, and is in fact morally bound to be above all a person without character; a man of character, on the other hand, a man of action, is mostly a fellow with a very limited imagination.

This is my conviction as a man of forty. I am forty now, and mind you, forty years is a whole lifetime. It is extreme old age. It is positively immoral, indecent, and vulgar to live more than forty years. Who lives longer than forty? I'll tell you who: clotheads and villains! I don't mind telling that to all old men face to face—all those silver-haired and ambrosial old men! I go about with tangled hair and often turn up unwashed in the most reputable of places; not out of poverty but out of vanity. My adversaries easily see through this, but inwardly I have no enemy and can thus put up with anyone with ease. Not long ago someone berated me because he felt like it. My serenity irritated him. One can almost do someone in by modesty. Irony can liberate as well as torment. I am one of those who have read Dostoyevsky.

Should readers of the above soliloquy acclaim it as vintage Walser, while others unfamiliar with Walser pronounce it, tentatively or confidently, as vintage Dostoyevsky of the early 1860s, there is excellent reason for either identification. This passage is made up of sequential portions of Walser's "The Child," interbraided with sequential portions of Dostoyevsky's *Notes from Underground* (1864). The Dostoyevskians, of course, will be seriously jolted by its last sentence, but would not put it quite beyond their author, bookish manipulator of book-ridden characters, to put himself on the soliloquizer's bookshelf, as he put Gogol's "Overcoat" (a seminal story for Dostoyevsky) in the hands of the old clerk, Devushkin, in *Poor Folk* (1846). Connoisseurs of Walser may be slightly taken aback by a more truculent tone in several passages than is common in Walser, and by a more conscious and aggressive alienation than marks

Walser's predominantly bemused and fastidious withdrawnness. But most readers would find disentangling the two authors from one another in the composite passage about as precarious as memorizing the subtle points of difference between identical twins, because a compelling need that is half arrogant demand, half self-effacing plea for respect and approval dominates their inner lives.

To whom, for another, shorter example, are we to attribute this:

In the past I used to be terribly distressed over appearing to be ridiculous. No, not appearing to be, but being. I have always cut a ridiculous figure, I suppose I must have known it from the day I was born. . . . And as during my studies, so all my life. . . . They always laughed at me, but no one of them knew or suspected that if there were one man on earth who knew better than anyone else that he was ludicrous, that man was I. And this—I mean the fact that they didn't know it—was the bitterest pill for me to swallow. . . . Oh, how I suffered in the days of my youth from the thought that I might not resist the impulse myself to confess it to my schoolfellows. But ever since I became an adult I have grown more composed in my mind for some reason. . . . Yes, most decidedly for some unknown reason. . . . Perhaps it was because I was becoming terribly disheartened by a particular circumstance that was beyond my power to control: the conviction that was gaining upon me that nothing in the whole world *made any difference*. . . . I suddenly felt that it made no difference to me whether the world existed or whether nothing existed anywhere at all. I started to be acutely aware that *nothing existed in my own lifetime* . . . that there had not been anything even in the past . . . that there would be nothing in the future either. It was then that I suddenly ceased being angry with people and almost stopped noticing them.

There are, as we know, unreleased fragments of Walser's writings in the Swiss *Nachlass*, and others may, or may have, come to light from other repositories. One may hope that the above fragment will yet be fitted to a context and intertext as nearly seamlessly as the underground man was a while ago to Walser's "Child."

# Cinderella

*Garden behind a house.*

CINDERELLA
>  That they would scold me unto tears
>  Won't make me cry, for what is bad
>  Is crying, not the reprimand.
>  If all that hatefulness of theirs
>  Won't make me cry, then hate is dear
>  And sweet as cake, while if I cried
>  It would be inky like a cloud
>  That meanly hides the sun from us.
>  No—if I did cry I would feel
>  A hatred so severe it might
>  Not be assuaged by tears alone.
>  Abomination that it is,
>  It would consume my life, it would
>  Devour my corpse. How lovely does
>  Its poison essence seem to me—
>  The cheerful girl who never cries,
>  Who has not tasted other tears
>  But those of happiness, of quite
>  Unthinking joy. I think there is
>  Some elf that in my senses dwells,
>  Who is a stranger to dark moods;
>  And when they make me cry it is
>  High spirits crying in me; when
>  They hate me, my good cheer loves back,
>  Inept at hating hate itself.
>  When they pursue me blind with rage
>  And with their anger's poisoned shaft,
>  I smile. My being radiates
>  Against their nature like the sun,
>  Though its gay beam may fail to find
>  Their souls, it may suffice to daze
>  Their wicked hearts for just a while.

And always busy as I am,
I have no time for weeping left—
Though much for laughing! Labor laughs,
The hands as they perform it laugh,
The soul laughs, being glad to do
What turns all men to friendliness,
Hard bitten though they be. Come, heart,
And laugh my discontent away.

*(She is about to leave. Her sister speaks from an upstairs window.)*

FIRST SISTER

The wench behaves as if she were
Worth looking at; she stands stock still
Like some proud column in the sun.
A feast for the observing eye.
Off to the kitchen, lazy slut,
Have you forgotten what few chores
You owe?

CINDERELLA

I'm on my way, be calm.
I merely paused, engrossed in thought,
As I came walking up just now.
I thought how beautiful you were
(And your dear sister); how each bears
Her face with such charm; and much more
That stirs my helpless envy up.
Your pardon, then, and let me be
Obediently on my way.

*(Exits.)*

FIRST SISTER

The witless butt of foolish dreams,
We are too kind to her, I think.
The slut laughs up her sleeve at us
But makes a long face when she is
Caught giggling in her crafty way.
From now on I will play the whip
To her well-calculated sloth.

The garb of toil shall cover her
In swirling swathes of dusty black;
Then let her dream of lovely looks,
The hypocrite, who only just
Stood idling; let me go at once
And see that she is given work.
*(She closes the window.)*

*Change of scene. An apartment in the royal palace.*
PRINCE

What can it be that saddens me?
Is it my mind that makes my self
A stranger to me? Is it guilt
That weighs upon my life? Or gloom
Received by me from nature? Grief
Is enemy to dulcet joy;
I feel it, grieving as I am.
In my sad state I feel it well.
But whence is this malign disgrace
Thrust down on the forsaken mind?
This neither reason can explain
Nor insight, its comrade in arms.
I dumbly bear it, just the way
Fate thrust it on me. —Music! Ah!
Whose pure and peaceful voice is this?
I kiss whosoever voice it is,
As, mystically, it kisses me.
To me in this sweet kiss resides
Appeasement. Grief has flown away.
This music now is all I hear,
A lovely dance is all I feel,
Which keeps communion with my limbs.
Does grief move with so light a step?
What grief? It's blown out of the door,
And I feel spendid once again.
The Fool?

FOOL

    The Fool, indeed, and always a fool,
    Fool of the Realm, Fool of the World,
    That very sweetheart of a fool,
    Who nothing ever was but fool,
    Quintessence of tomfoolery,
    Fool of a Monday, and no less
    Of Sature'en, fool in all things
    Fool for himself and for his lord,
    His Master's much devoted Fool.

PRINCE

    Tell me then, Fool, what sorrow is.

FOOL

    It is a fool; and he who yields
    His soul to it is no less fool.
    That you are sorrow's fool I read
    On your sweet-acrid countenance.
    Pshaw, you own youth scolds you a fool
    The Fool himself calls you a fool.

PRINCE

    Is there not cause for sorrow then?

FOOL

    You are yourself the cause of it,
    The soil of its exultant bloom,
    You are its swing, which cradles it,
    Its bed, on which it broadly sprawls.
    There is no other cause but you.

PRINCE

    How shall I flee from sorrow then
    If sorrow's vessel is my self—
    Which means that grief and I are one?

FOOL

    Is this up to the Fool to say?
    Shall sorrow rank so high, I ask,
    Above a cultured mind? You must
    Agree, it ill becomes your wit.

PRINCE

> I have been flogging my poor wit
> As never I laid whip upon
> A slack exhausted hound. And now
> It's down and never a wag from it.

FOOL

> Let us exchange our clothes, as it
> Seems to me; you be the Fool,
> And I will twist your foolish ear,
> You slap your brow, acknowledge idiocy,
> From deep below confront my wit,
> Which grants a smile. Are you in earnest?
> Have had your fill of royalty?

PRINCE

> If I were cheerful I should yield it.
> But as it is I would refuse
> To barter for your jingling cap
> Even that burden which I would
> So gladly be delivered of.

FOOL

> A-hunting go: a lively steed,
> The jubilation of the horns,
> And what high joys the pastime yields
> Will kill the torpor which you take
> For irremediable grief.

PRINCE

> So be it, I'll take your advice
> As fully as my father heeds
> The prudent Chancellor's advice
> When his own wisdom should appear
> Impaired to him. Come, follow me.
> I make my exit from this scene
> Quite in the manner of the Prince
> In classic theatre, and you, the Fool,
> Are Fool most truly cast today.
> *(Exit.)*

FOOL

> Yes, devil take it, that I well believe,
> And may it readily be thought of me.
> It's no especial flattery, at that.
> But come right down to it, it pleases me.
> The Fool is favored by a Prince
> From worry lest he be a Fool.
> I, not a Prince, am lord no less
> In the most genuine sense of the word
> Since I am master over wit.
> My wit does dominate my lord,
> Who must have fallen out of wit
> Just now when lifted by my wit
> To summits of his princeliness.
> Prince without Fool is like such wit
> As falls entangled head over heel;
> What fooldom can this be to me
> Which o'er its nature sits enthroned,
> Disdaining it—what sort of Prince
> Who stands in such need of his Fool.
> Yet what am I his Fool for but
> To stay around his foolishness?
> Come, Fool, and go to join the fool.

*Change of scene. Site of a rockslide in the wood.*
*Prince on horseback.*

PRINCE

> Down to the plain. Let it race by
> Like a storm-swollen watercourse.
> Trees topple sideways to the eye,
> The sky revolves, the entire world
> Seems like a joyous hunting ground,
> Like a sequestered park to me
> For noble huntsmen whose intent
> Outruns their actions' scope by far.
> What gay sweet pluck possesses me,
> How good I feel. It's bravery
> That buoys the laden spirit up

Matching a soaring bird's ascent.
I seem an image to myself
Lifeless and yet so full of life,
Calm and excited all at once,
Now wry, now sweet at a moment's turn.
A noble valor's image is
The carefree pastime of the chase,
Which I am serving with a heart.
The forest is my dear delight,
My ballroom, where the limbs rejoice
In exercise. The trees replace
The rugs and holstery for me
That line my father's hall of state.
How grandly they envelop me;
More glorious no dream could be,
Sweeter no picture ever wrought
By Art—kind deity—herself.
Day passes in a flash for me
When spent thus martially; time filled
So pleasurably is a treat
Which only passes by too fast.

*Change of scene. Spacious apartment, with a staircase up to a gallery. Cinderella and the first sister.*

CINDERELLA

Look down upon my faithfulness,
Look, do look. Oh, my mind is all
Prepared to serve your will alone.
It lies here like a fashion box
Already open, and attendance
Is curled inside like a new fur
To warm you. Oh, how warmly does
My heart beat in your service! Please
Hit me right smartly with your hand
If for the merest wisp of time,
Be it the winking of an eye,
I am remiss in serving you.

But that can't be, since after all
To serve is sweet delight for me.

FIRST SISTER

Dull kitchen wench, you are not worth
The whipping one should lay on you.

CINDERELLA

You know I'm always at your feet.
I am allowed to kiss your hand,
That gentle hand which never strikes
My face except in just reproof.
You seem to gaze at me with eyes
Bright as the sun. I am the earth
Which lives on its benign embrace
And never can do otherwise
But meet your rays in lovely bloom.
I am not lovely, to be sure,
For love is what I lack, you know—
My sister is the lovesome one;
But she is not as fair as dear,
Yet lovelier than kindness is.
What happiness for me to be
Employed as servant at her feet.

FIRST SISTER

Don't talk so much; you'd better use
The time you squander chattering
To stir yourself with greater zeal.
Take your black fingers off my dress!

CINDERELLA

If I must serve you zealously
And still am not to use my hand,
What will I do my duty with?
Would it were done by flights of thought,
There would be no occasion then
For dirty hands displeasing you.
Longing would help your garments on,
Would exquisitely wait on on you.
My heart would make a servant girl

Just delicate enough perhaps;
Zest would be toiling for you then:
But would this really do for you?

FIRST SISTER

Do shut your mouth, who do you think
Has ears for so much jabbering?

CINDERELLA

Who do I think—yes, quite—and yet
My tongue must keep a rapid beat
To match my hands, so that my zest
Keeps both together out of breath.
A word will leap out of my mouth
And tease the hand, and it in turn
Will lure the tongue's prize off again:
The merry words, which swiftly then
Speed up the hands twofold, as if
They too had fingers on them. Hand
And speech join in a kiss and are
Most tenderly in marriage linked.

FIRST SISTER

Sluggards, the two of them. And you,
Their mistress, most of all, so that
You're always asking to be slapped.
Off with you now.

*(Exit.)*

CINDERELLA *(calling after her)*

Beat me, oh do!

*(The Prince appears in the gallery overhead.)*

PRINCE

I do not know just how I chanced
Into this fairy tale; a drink
Was all I asked, as hunters do;
But these apartments here are such
That eyes can't see them and the mind
Won't apprehend them properly.
A shimmering wafts along the wall,
A fragrance scatters yellow roses;

There's back and forth as of a soul,
Which solemnly then holds my hand.
And I stand still as if bewitched;
My senses are beset by it;
Then the constraint grows loose again,
The ceiling sways, the gallery
Reels silently beneath my foot.
Confusion . . . oh, but down below
Some lovely movement is afoot;
I'll take it in for what it is,
However hard to grasp for me.

CINDERELLA
What means or manner can it be
That turns a circle here with me,
Turns my behavior to deceit,
This heart into a bowling game?
For feelings shuttle back and forth
Like playballs thrown about for fun,
And I, who was to hold them, am
Entangled in this game's delight.
This troubles me, and yet again
It's but of slight, minute, concern;
I laugh, yet in the laughter lies
An ominous earnest, which in turn
Gives rise in me to heartier laughs.
The earnest in my actions is
Perilous-comical, so that
Misfortune even has to smile,
Which I should think is hard to do.
No—when I wept I was the butt
Of grief and worry's ridicule.
I would much rather laugh them both
Into a dear and touching thing.
There will be time to spare for tears
When time itself will weep for me.

PRINCE (bending down over the balustrade)
Are you a fairy tale, sweet child?
Are your slim feet and hands so made

That, should one brush them with a touch,
Their splendor would dissolve in air?
I beg you like a supplicant:
Speak—are you vision, make-believe?

CINDERELLA

Sir! I am Cinderella. Look:
The dirt and soot upon my dress
Says so more clearly than my lips.

PRINCE

You are an angel; tenderness,
Confused about the sense of words,
Calls you an angel, stammering.
What else are you?

CINDERELLA

Oh, just a fibbing foolish thing,
Who'd like to know who *you* might be.

PRINCE

You grant reply, and take it back
By promptly asking in your turn.

CINDERELLA

No, no, don't tell. You are a prince,
Son of a king, as one can see
From certain antiquated ways
Uncompromising with our time.
There is the ermine cape, for one,
Draped from one shoulder down your back;
You bear a sword, too, and a lance,
A thing no longer done, I think.
So runs my thinking; but perhaps
I am mistaken; still, a prince
You are, that I feel certain of.

PRINCE

True—quite as surely as you are
My bride.

CINDERELLA

Did you say that I am your bride?
Don't talk like that! It gives me pain

To be made light of and unloved,
And by so fine a lad, what's more.

PRINCE

I see it now, the glittering crown
Pressed down into your hair—a sight
To which art is a fractious tool,
And Love abashed and at a loss.

CINDERELLA

Why did you come this way, and how?

PRINCE

This, Fairytale will tell you last;
When the dear story's lips at length
Silence has stilled, when voice and sound,
And color, din, and waterfall,
And lake and wood have disappeared.
When this occurs, the how will leap
Into your consciouness—and yet,
What I am here *for* I don't know.
Compassion, tenderness, these two
Are arcane spirits, after all,
Whose work no reason grasps. Be still,
Submit to the severe decree
Which is your lot. All this
Will be explained in proper course.

*(Cinderella falls into a state of drowsy musing. On the gallery
overhead appear the King and the Chancellor.)*

KING

Why, here we have the griffon bird,
Caught in our snare; but gripping him,
The rascal runaway, I see
With anger that it is my son.

PRINCE

Hush, father, do not move.

KING

I, not to move before the son
Who stands in blushes like a boy
Before my blame? Have you stepped forth

And I behind you, scamp, that you
Permit yourself this kind of speech?
Speak out now, by the lofty crown,
Tell how you came here, of all spots,
Just here! Out with it, spit it out,
The stammering confession, let
Me wrap my ears around it—Well?

PRINCE

With neither blush nor stammering
Can I oblige, as you expect;
With perfect calm, Sir, I report
To you, the realm, the world: I am
Betrothed.

KING

You are?

PRINCE

Yes, yes, betrothed in every sense
That ever language can express
And oath asseverate. That is
How fully I'm betrothed.

KING

My word! To whom?

PRINCE

A miracle who does not care
To be a miracle; the kind
Only a girl can be, and yet
Unheard of even as a girl.
Her sight has charm upon its knees
And rubbing its bedazzled eyes.
What's godly in this effigy
Is that it breathes and stirs with life,
And that she's mine, and I am hers.
This is a bond, my father, that
Is indissoluble—our blood
Would gush at parting; neither would
Live out the dearest love's demise.

KING
> Come, Chancellor, come!

PRINCE
> Oh let me kiss your hand, allow
> Love to petition at your feet!
> She, whom I would take unto me,
> In every sense deserves the throne.
> She will add luster to our house,
> Will be the joy of your old age.
> Oh do not chase the sunshine off
> That waits to warm your snow-white head!
> The maiden who enchanted me
> Is sure to charm and warm you too.

KING
> Be silent, will you? You don't know
> My mind towards you, after all!
> Listen, my son: though I may glare
> Like a wild bull, I don't propose
> To gore you just yet. Step with me
> Aside where it is black; in the dark
> We may exchange a word or two
> Which might smooth out our difference.

PRINCE
> Will you not meet with her before?

KING
> I've seen her in my mind, you know,
> I am won over in my dreams
> And nourish kindly thoughts of her.
> Which is not saying that the same
> Applies in reference to you.
> Come, step aside, and you will learn
> And grasp my fatherly intent.

*(They step more deeply into the gallery, so that only their heads remain visible.)*

CINDERELLA *(at the lower level, awakening)*
> Now I would like to know if I
> Can really pat it with my hands.

If it's a dream it comes to naught,
For dreams, however they may please,
Are surely worth no twinge or move.
Why don't I move my foot—like this—
And now a hand—and now my head.
The gallery from which that time
The sweetness hovered over me
Exists in sober, solid truth.
Although I cannot call to mind
Or ask somebody how it was
A prince bent down and spoke to me.
Whatever way, the matter is
Not lost so quickly, after all.
Perhaps it never came to be,
And I in my half drowsiness
Just dreamt it all a while ago.
And yet, that head, that smile do spell
A firm reality to me,
Which was before my sleep. Sleep has
Made me distrustful, shy to act,
And has destroyed the game in which
I was so blissfully engrossed.
Now let me try some forward steps,
To show myself I can still walk;
My gazes travel all around
And see that everything is clear,
By no means as mysterious
As I would like. Oh well, this thing,
All this, can wait, as I have said.
Here come the sisters.

*(Enter the two sisters.)*

FIRST SISTER
    Hey, Cinderella!

SECOND SISTER
    "Here," she will say, and "right away"
    Will be her idle sluggard's speech.

CINDERELLA

> Don't be annoyed, I am right here.
> Upon my kness, by your command,
> I'll kiss your hands and feet. So fast
> I never was prepared to serve,
> Nor liked to serve you, as today.
> Please tell me what I am to do.

SECOND SISTER

> Tie up the shoelace on this foot.

FIRST SISTER

> Go to the glovemaker for me.

CINDERELLA

> How gladly would I skip for you
> If tying did not tie me down.
> When I have tied, my zeal will fly
> To service for the sister who
> Commands my going. Once I am
> Back here, fatigue shall do no more
> Than brace itself to serve again.

SECOND SISTER

> Wench, you have laced it much too tight,
> You lazy lump. There, have for it!
>
> *(She pushes her away.)*

FIRST SISTER

> Go, off with you, and see you don't
> Loiter at corners or down lanes!

*(Exit Cinderella.)*

PRINCE *(on the gallery)*

> Is it not hate and envious pique
> That pompous pair of sisters spawn?
> How slim they are . . . they might look well
> Had not their nature been laid waste
> By dullness and pale jealousy.
> Yes—like invidious clouds they hang
> About the sun's sweet counterfeit,
> Their timid little sister, who

Surrenders to their bullying,
Seeing no recourse for herself.
They'd make a splendid fairy tale,
For children and for grownups too,
Those two clotheshorses à la mode
And their detested little fawn,
Detested for its very charm.
Where has it fled? Its nature is
Only too prone to leaps, I know,
I always fear it might escape.
Hoy, there, you sisters!

FIRST SISTER *(looking around)*
What does the yokel want?

SECOND SISTER
Mark this, you are too coarse for us.
Go, follow your ungentle trade,
Sic hounds on, wield the heavy spear,
Shoot hares dead—this is not the place
For such an uncouth servingman.

PRINCE
Yes, yes, enough said!

FIRST SISTER
Come, sister, leave the fool alone.

*(They converse in private. Cinderella enters unobserved.)*

PRINCE *(under his breath)*
O nightingale, you lovely dream,
Sweet apparition who excel
All dim imagination—look
How my two hands of their own will
Join into one to worship you!
One's language must be weasel-quick,
Hurtling beyond control at times
Lest it might lack expressive force;
But it admits its poverty,
Its lips by admiration sealed:
This is how love will bate one's breath.

CINDERELLA *(smiling)*
>Hush, whisperer, keep still!

PRINCE
>My father wants to see you sit
>Upon his lap as his crowned child.

CINDERELLA
>Is he an old man, then? Is he
>King of the Realm?

PRINCE
>Yes, yes, he is. I am his son.
>Just now he scolded me a scamp
>Who'd led him up the garden path
>By his big nose. Now he's all smiles
>And moistens both his cheeks with tears;
>But when I ask him why he cries,
>I turn into a guttersnipe,
>A cub lost to all decency,
>A felon of high majesty,
>A lout if ever one there was.
>So I stay quiet as a mouse
>And keep from breaking in on him
>While he is dreaming of your charm.

CINDERELLA
>And that he's doing this, of course,
>You, as a rascal, must not know?

PRINCE
>Exactly so.

CINDERELLA
>Go, hide yourself.

*(The Prince returns to his earlier position.)*

CINDERELLA
>All quietly, my angels laugh,
>Who ride the air above my head;
>They're pointing at the heads up there,
>Which are about half visible
>Above the balustrade: look up,

Mark, will you, the gigantic crown
Which so compels a merry laugh!
Take in the crisscrossed forehead there;
You next make out a young man's head
And toil at guessing who this is:
It certainly is not the Prince.
His head perhaps, but that won't work:
The upper half of any head
Can't surely be the head itself.
The nicest thing about this show
Is that the laughs must not be loud
But really low, so no one hears—
My sisters less than anyone;
They border on the ridicule
And are concerned in it, and yet
Unconscious of it. Yes, there lies
A slumber on the spacious hall,
Feeling is, as it were, confined
Within a casing. I, too, am
Fatigued beyond description now.
This column of the gallery
Shall be my cradle for a spell.

*(She leans against a pillar. Fairytale, in fantasy attire, enters behind the backs of the Prince and the King.)*

FAIRYTALE *(in a whisper)*
Cinderella!

CINDERELLA *(stepping forward)*
Now what is this? Who are you, speak!

FAIRYTALE
I'm Fairytale, out of whose lips
Comes forth all that is spoken here,
Out of whose hands the images
Which here enchant, go forth and pass,
Who in a moment may arouse
In you the sentiments of love
By lovely gifts designed for you.
Look here—these clothes will make of you

The fairest demoiselle and guide
The Prince's hand into your hand.
Look how it sparkles, how it gleams.
These precious jewels, corals, pearls
Are keenly longing to be yours,
Adorn your breast, gracefully chain
Your throat and arm. Come, take the gems
And with them take the dress itself!
*(She drops the dress from the balustrade.)*
If it should feel a trifle tight,
Be not disturbed—distinguished robes
Cling tightly to the limbs, they like
To hug the body avidly.
As to the shoes, I do believe
You have the little feet for them,
As delicate as they demand.
Would you not like the shoes as well?
*(She lifts them up.)*

CINDERELLA
You dazzle me.

FAIRYTALE
To startle you was why I came.
People do not believe in me;
No matter though, provided that
My coming stirs their thought a bit.
The shoes are silver, but as light
As swansdown; so look out and see
You catch them deftly in your hands.
*(She tosses them down into Cinderella's hands.)*

CINDERELLA
Oh!

FAIRYTALE
Don't tease your sisters with this sight.
Be noble with this noble pomp.
However, you conduct yourself
As inborn nature forces you.

CINDERELLA

Oh, I assure you.

FAIRYTALE

You are a dear and lovely child,
Fairytale-worth. Don't kneel to me!
Please, if you care for me, then kneel
To Him, to whom I kneel myself.

CINDERELLA *(kneeling)*

No, let me. It's from gratitude,
Who feels enriched by hands divine.

FAIRYTALE

It's for your mother's sake that I
Have come. One beautiful as she
Walks earth no more—one so adorned
With virtue that the latter was
Fairer than she, the prize—is dead,
Save possibly in you. You have
The sweetest that was hers, that which
Makes women godly—magic calm
Residing in a noble mind,
The inexpressible to which
Fine men will bend their knees. But hush!
Put on the dress in secret now,
Steal to the palace door at night;
The rest you know yourself—this was
Long enough dreamt. The scene must now
Pass on to lively change. Surprise
Shall now take fright, and Fairytale
Is making for the end, its home.
*(Exit.)*

CINDERELLA

Quick now, or else the sisters might
See me too soon, and I, too late,
Would mourn the loss. My mood would like
To linger here, but meets distrust
From one who's happy, and about
To flee now with her finery

And hide it. Mood, again, would like
To stay and smile, but happiness
The smiling one, laughs me away.
Quick, let the Prince not find me here!
*(Exit.)*

PRINCE

Ho, Cinderella!

KING

Come, it is night, let us go home.

PRINCE

I must be here forever.

*(Enter three girls dressed as pages.)*

FIRST PAGE

I feel so nervous in this dress
Which tries to make a boy of me.

SECOND PAGE

It tickles me, it tweaks, it stings,
I cannot name the feeling quite.
It kisses me all over, like.

FIRST PAGE

When first I pulled it on to me,
I felt a flame flare to my face.
Now, wearing it, I'm still not sure
If I shall come to terms with it.

THIRD PAGE

One wants to do just like the boys,
To skip and laugh, now here, now there,
And twist one's limbs—but finds no way.
There's something smothering, like a sin,
About my young white body now,
Which strikes me rigid.

FIRST PAGE

And yet, not for a kingdom's sake
Would I forgo the thrill of fear
The feeling brings. It feels so good
And so voluptuously sad.

    Heaven and earth—if heaven lay
    On top of earth but half as close,
    As tightly drawn as this array
    And I—they'd sense what it is like.

FIRST PAGE
    The Prince is calling, girls!

PRINCE
    What's this? What are you doing there?

FIRST PAGE
    We deck the setting, as your dream
    And as the fairy tale demands.
    We hang up costly draperies
    To decorate the gallery.
    Next come fine aromatic oils
    Which waft their fragrance through the hall;
    Now we light up the candlestands,
    And thus convert the chamber's night
    To shining day. If you have more
    Instructions for us, kindly name
    Your wishes.

SECOND PAGE
    Shall we halloo the people out
    Who are to clap the wedding feast?

PRINCE
    No, no, it's not the kind of fête
    Which needs the people, as you think,
    To make a frame of noise for it.
    We will conduct it by ourselves,
    We plan a very quiet feast,
    Lending the public's voice no board
    To roar against, and to the world
    Nothing to judge. Uncircumspect,
    We'll celebrate, without reserve
    Shall festive spirit swell our hearts.
    How could attending crowds but be
    Most burdensome of company,

Since they would shout for striking shows,
For idle pomp such as our joy
Has never yet partaken of.
I feel such quietness of joy,
Such a sweet sense of sacrament,
The very notion of a feast
Seems reprehensible to me.
I had been in a festive mood
Before you brought these candles here
To light the feast. Ambiguous Bliss,
Who, half rejoicing, half afraid,
Is like a tremor past all words,
Who doubts the happy outcome—she
Is mistress of the revels here.

THIRD PAGE

Just this last slender column here
Let me with bridal garlands deck.

PRINCE

But now do me the favor, go;
For best of service, best of thanks.

FIRST PAGE

A page of tact and breeding leaves
When there is no more need of him.

SECOND PAGE

Come, come, away. The Prince's page
Is reverie.

*(Exeunt pages.)*

PRINCE

I move so largely in a dream
I might as well submit wholesale
To alien power. Is what I see
Present itself before my eyes
My property? Or am I not
Placed into it as in a game?
How long I have been sitting here
While nothing would advance for me!
I fairly think myself deranged,

And everything around me here
No less so—and it comes about
By sorcery. Still, as I said,
I want to be enfettered, ruled.
My blood, as princely as it is,
Feels good when under such constraint,
And more than good. I'd like to shout,
With such a voice I'd like to shout
That over all the worlds the sound
Would, ebbing, travel. Oh, how good
One feels here through a "must," which else
Darkens the places where it reigns.
I've never looked as eagerly
Towards a magic dénouement.
The outcome of this matter here
Must be miraculous, since it
Makes me so anxious with suspense.
Ho, Father!

KING

I'm getting tired of this. Come home.

PRINCE

Here is my everlasting home.
I savor every moment like
A kiss; the onward glide of time
Touches my cheek caressingly,
My senses draw the fragrance in.
I cleave as closely to this word
As it to me. No, I will not,
Will never come away.

KING

What if I ordered you away?

PRINCE

You have here neither word nor power.
I'm pledged already to a word
And am commanded by a power
Which bids me pay no heed to you.
Forgive me, Father, there is now

A young rebellious urge in me
That you, too, must have known and felt
In your young days. Here I remain,
Waiting for life to stir again.

KING

I too must, I suppose. But don't
Mistake this for an outstretched hand
Extending pardon for your speech.

PRINCE

Forgiveness is so vastly sweet,
So dear to him who practices
It once, that I feel sure you will
Forgive me.

KING

Stuff and nonsense.

PRINCE

I will forget how strange I feel,
So even expectation will
Fall silent, and enquiry yet
Conceal its doings. After all,
I am in such a well-loved place
That patience should not come too hard.
All that alarms me is the thought
Of Cinderella's whereabouts.
What if she never came again,
If she entirely forgot
Where her emotions are to rest?
It is unlikely, to be sure,
But not absurd. The possible
Is quite a wide world, and things past
Which looked impossible before
*Were* possible, for they took place,
Though still enigmas to my mind.
Events unfathomed still occur,
As possible as in the past.
So be it. I'll be calm. We ought,
We males especially, be proud.

Yet how much fear is in the pride
So simulated! And such pride,
What is it worth before itself?
No—I will weep and mourn the chance
That keeps the child from me so long,
And I will trust that merely chance
It always be that does.

KING

I fear that while I dawdle here
In idleness, my kingdom quakes.
But let disorder wallow, now
The fairy tale's approaching end
Intrigues me. Later on I can
Resume the god of order's role.
Government, too, enjoys a snooze
Once in a while; the Source of Law
Is only human, too.

PRINCE

I'd hold my breath most willingly
To hark more keenly for her step;
For she has such a gentle tread
That even intuition fails
To mark her coming. Would that she
Did now approach the avid mind,
Which fairly makes its fibers part
To feel her near. How sweet it is,
That closeness, when what is concerned
Is that we love, and how uncouth
When wickedness intrudes on us.
Right here is where a lovely thing
Should urge and clamor, but this is
Precisely what love's way is not.
He's silent where he must forget;
He hasn't that resounding voice
Which marks bad faith. Oh, he is rich
And does not stand in need of words
To have himself remembered. Far,

So very far my love cannot
Be distant now, thus feeling tells
Me vividly. All I can hope
Is that patience will not forsake
Him who so waits. I must stand here—
This is as firmly anchored as
Ever authority decreed.
Lovers like waiting, for their dream
Of the belovèd forces time
To trembling haste. For what is time
But bickering impatience, which
Is now allayed. What glitters there?
*(He descends the stairs from the gallery.)*

KING

I cannot properly make out
Why I am getting wedded here
To silence. I would think I am
Too old for marriage. Reason scolds,
Pointing a finger at me, hoots
With laughter, but what does that mean!
I'm up in years and have a right
To foolishness. Yes—tolerance
Walks merrily a common path
With snowy hair. I tolerate
My son's bold guardianship of me.
From whimsy (which we know attends
Old age, cavorting) I comply
With what the mind of youth resolves.
I sleep. —Fatigue suits my white hair
As well as slumber does befit
Headshaking senile reasoning.

PRINCE *(below, with the single shoe in his hand)*
I would regard this object as
A prelude to approaching splendor
And love. It is a shoe which takes
A delicate foot to wear, bespeaks
A girl of breeding, just as though

It had a mouth, and eloquence.
Not to the stony sisters there
Can this frail ornament belong;
How could they have the foot to match
The narrow molding of this shoe?
Who owns it then? This question, though,
I am not anxious to confront.
It awes me. Could it really be?
Could it be Cinderella's? —No;
The notion gives me needless pain.
Who'd give her gold and silver here,
Give her this royal jewelry?
And yet an inkling hints in me
At Cinderella, points to her
Antic demeanor, distant air,
And general manner. Sorcery
Is not to be ruled out, I know.
I hope for it, because there is
No grasping, holding it for me.

*(He pensively ascends the stairs. On top stands Cinderella in her maid's clothes, carrying Fairytale's gift in her arms.)*

CINDERELLA

So you are still about, my Prince?

PRINCE

Enchanting child, that I'm still here
Is just to see you once again.
What are you carrying?

CINDERELLA

Look, lovely clothes! Just feast your eyes
And look your fill; a royal eye
May well rejoice in them.

PRINCE

Who gave them to you?

CINDERELLA

Oh, you would hardly want to know;
I'm really not so sure myself.
Suffice it that the splendor's mine,

And I could wear it any time
I felt like it. Yet . . .

PRINCE

Yet?

CINDERELLA

I have stopped wanting to.

PRINCE

And why are you so strangely cold?
Who has disturbed your soul's clear lake?
With mud and darkened it like this?

CINDERELLA

I did myself, so please be still
And pocket your exalted ire;
There's no offense in question here.
Only . . .

PRINCE

What? Tell me, dearest!

CINDERELLA

There is one thing that irks me still,
And that is that this pretty set
Is short one piece. It's the left shoe
I find it missing . . . ah, this is,
This is the one.

PRINCE

Well yes—and is it yours?

CINDERELLA

How can you ask, since after all
It is the other's perfect twin?
So now I have the splendid gift
Complete again and can depart.

PRINCE

Depart so as to put it on
The enchanting body, I presume?

CINDERELLA

No, not that!

PRINCE
   What ails you of a sudden?
CINDERELLA
   So sudden, yes . . . what can it be?
PRINCE
   You have stopped loving me?
CINDERELLA
   I do not know if I love you.
   I love you, there's no doubt of it,
   For what young girl is not in love
   With high estate and bravery,
   With handsome, noble bearing matched?
   I love your splendor, which is so
   Devotedly awaiting me.
   I'm touched that, of all people, you
   Should cherish, of all people, me.
   I am so quickly touched, so swift
   To feel excited; truth to tell,
   I live quite wretchedly exposed.
   Just any little puff of wind
   Whips up a tempest in my soul,
   Only to have it fall as still
   As now it lies outspread, a lake
   At rest and shining in the sun.
PRINCE
   Your nature is indeed like this?
CINDERELLA
   Like this or different. What can
   A word convey? Our sounds of speech
   Are all too coarse for things like this.
   It would take Music to repeat
   Them better: she would sound them forth.
(Music.)
PRINCE
   Listen—what charming dance music!
   A longing rises, swells my heart,
   And I can't bear our standing here

Much longer, hesitating. Come,
Let me conduct you to the dance.
Here is a feast held, opened up
To us by magic. Rid yourself
Of heavy silver freight, and come.

CINDERELLA

What, in this dress, my Lord, full of
Repulsive stains and dirt? Would you
Dance with a kitchen apron, hug
Sweepings and soot in close embrace?
I surely would reflect before
Playing this game.

PRINCE

Not I.

*(He carries her down the stairs. Arrived below:)*

So dance a princely pair.

*(They dance. After a few phrases the music falls silent.)*

CINDERELLA

See! See!

PRINCE

As if it warned us to be still!

CINDERELLA

That *is* her will. She is the soul
Of delicate feeling, and dislikes
Sound to be muted by the dance.
Vivaciously she points us to
Imagination: don't we dance
In dreams as well as waking? Dance
Must not be danced here, that is, thumped.
Feeling is sensitive enough
Even to dance without one foot
And noiselessly. Hush—let us hear
What else Music intends for us.

*(Music resumes.)*

PRINCE

Listen—sweet as a dream.

CINDERELLA

    She, as a dream, you see, contrives
    Subtly to stir the dream in us.
    She does not thrive in open space,
    Takes refuge in a silent realm
    Where none but she will set the air
    Vibrating gently. Let us plumb
    Her contents thoroughly. This done,
    Let us forget what after all
    Must be forgotten. Let us trace
    The trail of sensibility
    Which in the crush of common things
    We lost. Nor shall we easily
    Discover that sweet thing. One needs
    Infinite patience—hardly given
    To human mind. It is as though
    We meant to comprehend, first try,
    The inconceivable. Instead,
    Let's cheer up and relax.

PRINCE

    As sweet as music sounds your speech.

CINDERELLA

    Hush, don't break in upon the thought
    Which, half released, pains me so much.
    When it is free, I will be gay
    And happy just as you demand.
    Yet it will never leave its jail,
    The mind—I feel this in my heart
    With sharp resentment. No, it will
    Die like a sound, timid, in debt;
    And never will its memory die.
    A part will stay alive in me—
    Unless I am redeemed by chance.

PRINCE

    What thought is this that preys on you?

CINDERELLA

    Oh, nothing, just a whim.

If we decided to pursue
Each trifle so, why . . . fiddlesticks—
We'd find no end to it, of course,
For start and mid and end are quite
Disjointed members which as yet
No mind has grasped, and never a heart
Has felt. What it comes down to is
I'd like a happy time with you.

PRINCE

Oh, how you touch me and enchant
With your uncalculating way,
Which, judging by all signs it gives
Is nobly bred. But let us now
Forget both who and what we are,
Share gaiety as we did fear
Fair and alike. You do not speak?

CINDERELLA

No—quite the captive nightingale,
Which cowers with trembling in the snare
And has unlearnt her melodies.

PRINCE

You flatter me!

CINDERELLA

All yours I am, so shyly yours
That I must ask my body back
To go deep into hiding there.

PRINCE

I give a royal realm to you . . .

CINDERELLA

No, no!

PRINCE

A house for you to live in which
Is deeply bedded in a park;
Your gaze will rest upon the trees,
On flowers, on serried shrubbery,
On ivy garlanding the wall,
And on the sky which favors you

With sunlight grander than the rest,
Because it filters through the green;
The lunar ray is finer there;
The tender spruce-tip tickles it
To soreness point. The calls of birds
Provide a concert for your ears,
Lovely past words. You calmly move
As mistress through the artful park
By pathways which, as if they had
Discernment, will part company
And suddenly combine again
In one. Tall fountains cheer you there,
You dreamer, when you sink too deep
In brooding thought. All things, in short,
Are there to serve you, any time
It pleases you to feel it all
Beneath you there and, all serene,
Rule over it.

CINDERELLA

You make me glad! Isn't it true,
I'd feel like someone doted on
Like child in arms? Your arms, I know,
I'd nestle up to and feel blessed.
The clothes you see here, though, with which
I am so wretchedly in love,
These I would have to part with then,
Could Cinderella be no more . . .

PRINCE

You will have maids to wait on you
And wardrobes full of lovely clothes.

CINDERELLA

I will?

PRINCE

All day you would be left in peace
And to yourself; and only if
A need for people and more noise
Than offers your retreat should drive

You from your park, the palace would
Hold noisy fun enough, bright pomp,
Dance, music, raving, all for choice.

CINDERELLA

This would in turn make solitude
Seem dear and lovely once again
By contrast—am I right?

PRINCE

Exactly.

CINDERELLA

How dear you are. I cannot find
In all the borderless domain
Of gratitude one little word
Of thanks to you. So, failing all
Thanks-rendering, let me instead
Kiss you—like this. Oh, that was sweet!
A good thing that it's over now.

PRINCE

Over? What's over?

CINDERELLA

The frolicking is over now,
The dance with me. I am betrothed
Still to myself and not to you.
Memory warns me that as yet
I have not fully dreamt dear things
That waft about me here and there,
That leave me much to see to yet.
You see the silent sisters there
Who stare at us dumbfounded, just
As if they had been turned to stone.
I pity them, although by rights
They merit no compassion. But—
It's not the true sort, anyway;
It's for my own sake what I feel.
I love the two, who are so strict
And harsh with me—I am in love
With punishment I don't deserve,

With angry speeches, for the chance
To smile serenely. This affords
An inexhaustible delight,
Fills up the lengthy day for me,
And keeps me jumping, noticing,
Reflecting, dreaming. For at heart
A dreamer's really what I am.
I'd be too rashly pledged to you,
Who's worthy of a better girl.
The fairy tale won't let it be.

PRINCE

It wills it! It's the fairy tale
That wants to witness us betrothed!

CINDERELLA

The dreamy goings-on here make
A merrier fairy tale than that.
With you I could not dream!

PRINCE

You could! You could!

CINDERELLA

No, were it placed before me so—
Like food before a captive bird—
I could not hug it to myself,
I could not kiss it.

PRINCE

You want to see it in its flight.
It is to cost you effort hunting
It down; you'd only want a dream
If you had had to catch it on the wing?

CINDERELLA

How tenderly you read me! Yes.
Precisely so.

PRINCE

Oh well. Now calm yourself. I know
You'll go and put the dress on now,
Which Fairytale has granted you.
Such sweetness was ordained to you;

You won't escape the bondage though
Ten thousand goblins in yourself
Dug in their heels. May I
Escort you to the door?
*(They rise.)*
Look—would you want to waste yourself?
The natural breeding that is yours
Predestined you to be my spouse.
You weep?

CINDERELLA
Because I have to follow you,
And notwithstanding what was said
Will follow you so gladly.

PRINCE
I pray you will, most earnestly.
*(Exit Cinderella with the clothes she has gathered up.)*
Ho, Father!

KING *(from above)*
Son, what a girl this is!

PRINCE
I take it she will do?

KING
I'll see she shall ascend the throne
As goddess. Her ascension shall
Arouse the land with music and
Festivity. I shall straightway
Proclaim the matter to our state.
She in the meantime should, with you,
Follow the cloud of jubilant cheers
Which, incense-like, will roll ahead.
*(Exit King.)*

PRINCE
I will await her coming here.
*(to Cinderella, who appears on the gallery in
the costly attire)*
Ah—you are here!

CINDERELLA
   At your command, my Lord.
PRINCE
   Oh, you! How can one . . .
   *(He rushes to the stairs to meet her.)*
CINDERELLA
   I will, I will.
                    (1901)   Trans. W.A.

# Snowwhite

QUEEN

> Child, are you ill?

SNOWWHITE

> Why ask me that? You, after all,
> Wish death on her who always stung
> Your eyes by being over fair.
> Why such a gentle gaze for me?
> The kindness which so lovingly
> Wells from your eye is only sham,
> The kindly tone to order made.
> Hate is what dwells within your heart;
> Did you not send the huntsman out
> And bid him raise his falchion high
> Against the abominated face?
> Have I been taken ill, you ask?
> Scorn ill becomes such winsome lips.
> Yes, kindness turns to wicked scorn
> When it deals wanton cruel wounds.
> I am not ill; why, I am dead!
> That poisoned apple hurt so much,
> Oh, oh, so much, and Mother, you,
> You were the one who brought me it.
> And now you mock my being ill?

QUEEN

> Love, you mistake me. You *are* ill,
> Yes, gravely, really gravely ill.
> The wholesome garden air, no doubt,
> Will do you good. I beg of you,
> Bruise not your troubled little head
> On any thoughts. Be quite at peace,
> Stop brooding over this or that,
> Seek exercise, go jump and run,
> Hail and pursue the butterfly,

Abuse the air, berate it as
Not warm enough yet. Be a child
And you will soon have lost that hue
That overcasts your rosy face
Like a pale shroud. Think on no sin,
The sin shall be forgotten. Years ago
I may have sinned in your regard;
Who'd trouble now to bring that up?
Unpleasant things, you know, the mind
Forgets with ease when it can think
Dear things close by. What! Not in tears!

SNOWWHITE

In tears, yes! I must cry to hear
That you would break the neck of what
Went by so swiftly as you meant
To wring my own neck. Cry? Why not—
Mourn culpable forgetfulness
Which aims to flatter. Oh, like this
You harness wings to sin, and yet
It flies ill with the new-rigged pair
Which does not fit. It roosts too near
To me, and you, for you to try
To jolly it off with blandishment;
So near, I say, so touchable near
That it will never leave my mind,
Nor will you, who committed it.
Huntsman—did you not vow my death?

HUNTSMAN

Indeed, Princess, swore deadly blow,
Yet dealt it not—as loud and true
The fairy tale confirms, you know.
What moved me was your touching plea,
Your countenance, sweet as the snow
Beneath the kiss of the sun.
I sheathed what was to murder you;
Then plunged it in the deer that chanced
To cross our path just then. I sucked

Its blood up with a ravenous will
But left your own untapped . . .
Say not, therefore, I vowed your death,
For, pitying, I broke the vow
Before I ever did you harm.

QUEEN

There, then. Why are you crying so?
He raised the dagger just in jest;
To stab at you, he would have had
To stab his own compassion first;
So he refrained, for kindness lives
Fresh in him like the sparkling sun.
Give me a kiss, come, and forget,
Let's see a bright eye, and good sense.

SNOWWHITE

How? How am I to kiss these lips
Whose kisses spurred the hunter on
To brutish deed? I'll never kiss you.
It was with kisses, after all,
That you inflamed this hunter here
And death was mine the instant he
Became your sweet and best beloved.

QUEEN

What's this you say?

HUNTSMAN

She . . . me? With kisses?

PRINCE

I really think it must be true.
This man in the green coat does seem
To stand in less awe than is fit
Before the Queen's high majesty.
O Snowwhite—what a wicked game
Did callous hatred play with you!
A wonder that you are alive.
Both knife and poison you withstood.
What stuff can you be fashioned of?
You're dead and yet too touchingly

Alive; indeed, so little dead,
The living fall in love with you!
Tell: did this huntsman stab at you?

SNOWWHITE

No, no, in this man's bosom beats
A feeling and compassionate heart
If but the Queen had such a heart
She'd be a better mother to me . . .

QUEEN

I have your good much more at heart
Than wild distrust suggests to you.
I never launched this huntsman forth
To you by kisses. Mindless fear
Has led you to suspect all this.
The truth is that I all along
Have loved you as my pure, dear child.
Where would be cause, and grounds, and right
For me to hate you, whom I cherish
Just like a child of my own breast!
Oh, do not trust the craven voice
That whispers sin which is not there.
Oh, trust the right and not the left—
I mean the false—ear which presumes
To make the wicked mother of me,
Envious of beauty. Come, do not
Pay heed to the preposterous yarn
Which pours into the world's all too
Receptive ear the news that I
Am crazed with jealousy, by nature bad—
While all of it is empty talk.
I love you. No confessing has
Confessed more genuinely yet.
Your beauty only makes me glad,
Beauty in one's own daughter is
Like balm to mother's flagging joy,
Not goad to such repulsive deed
As fantasy has underlaid

This fable here, this spectacle.
Don't turn away, be a dear child,
Trust parent word like your own self.

SNOWWHITE

Oh, I'd be happy to believe,
Since to believe is quiet bliss.
But with how much belief can I
Believe where no belief can be,
Where roguish malice lies in wait,
Where proud injustice stiff-necked sits?
You speak as gently as you can,
But cannot act as gently yet.
The eye which glints with so much scorn
Darts down to me so dire with threat,
Unmotherlike, and grins with doom
Behind your tongue's endearing notes—
Which it disdains: it tells the truth,
And I believe it, that proud eye
Alone, and not the treacherous tongue.

PRINCE

I find your trust well placed, my child.

QUEEN

Must you keep adding, little prince,
More fuel yet unto these flames
Where healing floods is what we need?
Mind, piebald stranger, mind you don't
Trespass upon a queen's domain.

PRINCE

What, monstrous woman, would I not
Dare for the Princess's dear sake?

QUEEN

What?

PRINCE

Indeed; I may seem small and weak,
But I'll repeat a thousand times,
Ten, hundred thousand times to you:

A wicked crime has here occurred,
And witness points to you, the Queen.
For poison meat was flung before
This lovely child as to a dog.
Why? Let your malice tell you that,
Your easy conscience! Come, sweet child,
Let's go indoors for a short spell
And ponder over this our grief.
If you feel weak, just lean your weight
Upon this trusty shoulder here,
Which will rejoice in such a load.
We beg to leave you, Queen, meanwhile
To that short span of time.
*(to Snowwhite)*

                         Please come,
Allow me this sweet liberty.
*(He escorts her into the palace.)*

QUEEN

Begone, then, torn-up rigging you.
Go, bridal pair, to death betrothed.
Go, grief, take puniness in tow
And lovey-dovey arm in arm.
Come, tender huntsman, let us chat.

*Change of scene. A chamber in the palace. The Prince
and Snowwhite.*

PRINCE

I'd gladly spend the livelong day
Just talking, arm in arm with you.
Oh, how it acts on me, the speech
That issues from your lovely lips!
How merry is your word alone.
Enraptured by its wealth, my ear
Hangs in a hammock, as it were,
Of heark'ning, dreams of violins,
Of lispings, nightingales' sweet sobs,
Love twitterings. And now and then

Against our garden's margin drift
Dream ripples like the lake's light surf.
Oh, speak, and I am wrapt in sleep,
And thus a prisoner of love,
Hobbled, yet infinitely rich,
Free as no freeman yet was free.

SNOWWHITE

You speak high-minded princes' talk.

PRINCE

No, let me listen, so the love
I swore to you down in the park's
Green pleasances shall never waft
In idle words away from me.
I would but listen and within
Respond unto your note of love.
Speak, so that *I* may ever be
Silent and true to you. Forsworn
Is quick with words; it speaks as fast
As a spring in the wind that lashes it,
And bubbles over babbingly.
No—let me silence keep, and faith with you.
This understood, I love you more
Than just with loving. Tenderness
Ceases to know itself then, showers
Moisture upon me, as on you.
Let love be humid as the night,
Lest ever arid dust perturb it.
Speak, then, so that your speech, like dew,
May trickle down upon our love.
You are so still! Where are you looking?

SNOWWHITE

Why, *you* talk like a waterfall
Of silence, which you do not keep.

PRINCE

What ails you—speak! You look so gravely,
So wretchedly down at your toes
As if you sought the language there

That whispers love. Be not distressed,
Speak out if something weighs on you,
Spread it face upward like a rug
On which we'll then disport ourselves.
On heartache it's such fun to frolic.

SNOWWHITE

You are still talking, though you pledged
Silence a while ago. Why talk
Continually and in such haste?
Trust does not know such rapid speech,
And love is fond of downy rest.
Oh, if you are not dedicated
To my delight in every way,
Then say so, please. Speak, for you said
Betrayal used such busy talk,
So glibly spoke bad faith alone.

PRINCE

Oh drop this, please.

SNOWWHITE

Yes, let us chat, be cheerful, let
Low spirits and all paltry woe
Be banished from the realm of love.
What care we for the ills of Time,
Who would command us to be mute!—
Something to see there in the park?

PRINCE *(looking out of the window)*

Ah—what I see is dear and sweet
To just the eye, which merely gazes;
It's holy to the sense which captures
The picture in its subtle nets.
But to the mind which knows the past
It's ugly like the turbid flow
Of muddy water. Ah, the sight
Is of two kinds, lovely and bad,
Provocative and sweet. Come here
And look at it with your own eyes.

SNOWWHITE

      No, *you* tell it. What do you see?
      And I will gather from your lips
      The picture's subtle lineaments.
      When you depict it, I am sure,
      You'll soothe the harshness of the view
      With judgment wise and shrewd. Well? Start.
      I'd like to hear instead of watching.

PRINCE

      It is the sweetest sensual glow
      That ever kindled loving pair;
      The Queen kissing the huntsman's lips,
      And he returning kiss for kiss.
      They sit beneath the willow tree
      Whose pendent trailers wave and brush
      At either head. The grass embraces
      The knot of intertangled feet.
      The planking groans beneath the weight
      Of the two bodies turned to one
      In their ecstatic bliss of love,
      Oh, thus a pair of tigers love
      Deep in the jungle, world-forlorn.
      The sweet delight which makes them one
      Tears them apart, only the more entranced
      To give themselves again. I am
      Speechless and imageless before this scene.
      Care you to see it and be speechless too?

SNOWWHITE

      No—it would turn my stomach. Come,
      Away from the repulsive sight.

PRINCE

      The magic of its colors scarce
      Will let me loose. It is a scene
      Which surely has sweet love for painter.
      How she is lying there, the Queen,
      Fair crushed in his encircling arms
      How she cries out with passion now,

That yokel staunching her with kisses;
This is how lid is put on dish,
No, on a heaven, for heavenly delight
Is surely what this mouth encloses.
That rascal is quite impudent,
He thinks his forester's green suit
Saves him from stabs. Ah, I call stabbing
What so entranced gleams up to me.
I am delirious—oh, that woman!
If only I could lose the mind
That took this in. Now I am lost.
Tempest is sweeping over all
That once was love, still wants the name,
But bears it not. Away with it!

SNOWWHITE

Alas for me that I must hear . . .

PRINCE

For both, what I was made to see!

SNOWWHITE

Oh, I want nothing more, you see . . .
Than to be dead and smiling; dead.
That's what I am, too, always was.—
I've never known hot gusts of life.
I am as still as yielding snow
Which lies supine for rays of sun
To take it up. Thus I am snow
And melt beneath the warming breath
Which wafts for spring and not for me.
Sweet is the seeping off. Dear Earth,
Receive me in your dwelling house!
I hurt so underneath the sun.

PRINCE

Is it my doing, this sharp ache?

SNOWWHITE

Oh, no, not yours. How could it be!

PRINCE

How dear you are! The smile you give me,

The laugh you offer! Love me not,
I only undermine your peace.
Oh, had I only left you there!
How fair you were, so still and white,
Like snow upon the wintry world.

SNOWWHITE

Snow? Always snow?

PRINCE

Forgive me, winter image dear,
Likeness of pious white repose!
If I offended you, it was
Done but in Love. Now Love, in tears,
Averts his face from you again
Towards the Queen. And pardon Love
For lifting you from that glass vault
In which you lay and rested then,
With cheeks like roses, open lips,
And semblance of a living breath—
That was a sight sweet unto death:
Would only I had left it so,
Then love would kneel before you still.

SNOWWHITE

Well, well! . . . Now that I am alive
You cast me off as if I weren't!
How strange you men are, to be sure.

PRINCE

Do scold me, hard; it pleases me.
Hate me, and I'll drop on my knees
To you. Call me a worthless knave:
It shall be boon to me. But now
Let me seek out the lovely Queen,
Whom I intend to liberate
From an unworthy love. Please be
Right angry, right enraged with me.

SNOWWHITE

Why should I, though? Do tell me why?

PRINCE

    Because I am the kind of brute
    That throws you over for another
    More teasing to his mind—that's why.

SNOWWHITE

    No, never a brute! So that is it! . . .
    More tempting to your mind, your sense?
    What pack of hounds incites your sense
    So that, affrighted like a doe,
    You flee before the enemy
    Who chases you. Still—let it be.
    Flee from me then, run to the brook
    Which slakes your thirst with better drink.
    I'll stay and smile, enticing you
    By reaching out with pallid arms.
    I'll trace your flight with merry voice,
    Which calls "Snowwhite's awaiting you,
    Come here and knock at the old door,"
    And laugh aloud. Then you will turn
    Your dear and faithful head to me
    And will implore me to be still,
    For screaming was no use. Do go!
    I wish you'd go now; I dismiss you.
    My humble duty to my Queen.

PRINCE

    Your humble duty to the Queen?
    How . . . am I dreaming?

SNOWWHITE

    What *is* it? Am I not allowed
    To give you greetings for Mamma,
    Who's down there in the shady park,
    Engaged in some embroidery?
    Some needlework to do with love—
    Not my affair. I owe her love,
    And love will greet her thus through you.
    Say I forgive her . . . rather, no.
    As things stand now, it would not be

Exactly fitting for a child.
Seek pardon for me on your knees,
You will be kneeling anyway
For your own love's sake. Work it in
As a sweet tidbit on the side,
And take due note how graciously
She'll nod, in strained emotion leave
Her hand to your consuming kiss,
And, since you were so well behaved,
Send me forgiveness for my fault.
How I impatiently await
My mother's word! Do hurry off.

PRINCE

Snowwhite—I cannot make you out.

SNOWWHITE

That's neither here nor there, you know.
Go now, I ask you. Leave alone
The flower which shows its fullest bloom
To solitude alone. It was
Not meant for you in any case.
Therefore be calm. Surrender me
To dreaming here, which gorgeously
Unfolds like an exotic plant.
Go to the other flower, be off
And sip a sweeter nectar there.

PRINCE

Compose yourself, and tarry here.
I'll bring the Queen back here for you
All reconciled. In just a while
I'll seek her in the shady park.
Of that foul hunter I'll demand
A reckoning, when, where, and how
I may encounter him. Till then
Be calm and wait for her return
*(Exit.)*

SNOWWHITE

He is all restless, and commends

Repose to me, which clearly has
A deeper hold on me than him.
Let all go forward as it must.
The Prince's breach of faith does hurt,
But I don't cry; as I would not
Be jubilant if now I had
Proof of his most devoted love.
I do not care to act out more chagrin
Than does chagrin, and it stays mute
And gulps its fear down, which is what
I do myself. Aha—here comes
Mamma herself, and quite alone.
*(to the Queen who enters)*
O kindly Mother, pardon me.
*(She flings herself to her feet.)*

QUEEN

What *is* this? Do get up, my child.

SNOWWHITE

No, on my knees before you—thus.

QUEEN

What is amiss? What moves you so,
What is that tremor in your breast?
Get up and tell what troubles you.

SNOWWHITE

Do not withdraw the gentle hand,
I want to cover it with kisses.
How I was longing for this touch!
Squirming excuses do not plead
So anxiously to be forgiven
As I do here. Forget, forgive,
Let you be my indulgent mother,
And me the child of your kind heart,
Who shyly nestles at your waist.
O sweet hand, I suspected you
Of fell design upon my life,
Proff'ring the apple: it's not true.
Sin is so subtly engineered

By multifarious thought alone.
Yes—thinking is the only sin
Existing here. Absolve me, please,
Of the distrust which hurts you so.
To love you,—love,—is all I want.

QUEEN

What? Was the huntsman never sent?
Did I not spur him on with kisses
To do the sinful, sinful deed?
Think how your thinking goes awry.

SNOWWHITE

I only feel! And feeling's thought is shrewd,
It is awake to every point
Of this affair. And by your leave,
Feeling conceives more nobly far
Than thinking does of any case.
Its judgment, bare of any judging,
Judges more shrewdly—simply too.
So I don't hold with thinking much,
It pores and ponders back and forth,
Full of grave airs and lofty view,
Says "It was thus" and forces down
A petty verdict of damnation.
Off with the judge who only thinks!
Not feeling, he will think minutely,
His judgment has the stomachache,
It's pale and drives the plaintiff mad,
Acquits the sinner all the more
Of sin and voids the whole complaint,
All in the same breath. Go and fetch
That other justice here for me,
Sweet all-unknowing feeling bring,
Hear what it says. Why, not a thing!
It smiles and kisses sin to death,
Treats it to sisterly caress,
With kisses strangles it. My feeling
Declares you free of any sin,

It kneels in suppliant entreaty
Before you, begging: call me sinner,
Me, who so tensely sues for pardon!

QUEEN

I sent the poisoned apple down,
You ate of it and died, you know.
Dwarves kept you in the catafalque
Of glass till by the Prince's kiss
You were brought back to life.
This is what happened, is it not?

SNOWWHITE

But for the kiss, it is all true.
These lips have never yet been kissed
By desecrating lips of man.
How could the Prince have kissed, at that?
No hair yet grows on his smooth cheek.
He's but a little boy as yet,
High bred, indeed, but precious small,
Weak as the body he inheres,
Small as the sense he cherishes.
About a prince's kiss, Mamma,
Say nothing more. The kiss is dead
As if it never had perceived
The moistening touch of lip to lip.
What did I mean to speak of? Yes—
Transgression fallen on its knees
Before the dear transgressor, you.

QUEEN

No, that is false, you tell yourself
A lying tale. The story goes
That I am the ill-natured Queen,
Who sent her huntsman after you
And brought you poisoned fruit to eat.
Now make precise response to this.
It is to mock me that you ask
Forgiveness from me, is it not?
All this is studied mime and move,

Shrewdly premeditated speech?
I must say, you have rendered me
Suspicious now. What's in your mind?

SNOWWHITE

To gaze at this mild, kindly hand,
Look at its beauty, wondrously
Stirring emotions in a child
That were all but extinct before.
No—you are not a sinner; how
Could you have found the mind for it?
Nor am I one. We are as yet
Unstained by any shamefulness.
Look purely up to the pure sky,
Do good, as we are doing now.
We may have done each other harm,
But that occurred too long ago
For us to know. Open your lips—
Your dear lips—and, I beg of you,
Tell me the merriest thing you can.

QUEEN

I issued word for you to die,
Spared neither kisses nor caresses
For him who was to track you down,
Who chivied you like forest game
Through woods and meadows, till you dropped.

SNOWWHITE

Oh yes, I know that tale, and more,
That of the apple, the glass shrine.
Tell something else, oh be so kind.
Does nothing other come to mind?
Are you so fond of those devices
You cannot stop redrawing them?

QUEEN

With kisses, kisses did I spur
The hunter, no, the killer on.
To think how my caresses rained

Like dewdrops down upon the face
Which swore me faith, and doom to you.

SNOWWHITE

Forget this, if you please, dear Queen.
Give it no thought, I beg of you.
Roll not those big eyes as you do.
Why are you shaking? All your life
You did nothing but good to me,
I feel such gratitude for you—
If love knew better words it might
Discourse less clumsily, perhaps.
Love, on the other hand, is boundless,
Is poor at speech because it is
So wholly wrapped up in yourself.
Hate me, enabling me to love
But the more childishly, the more
For the impulsive warmth alone.
And for no other reason but
That love itself is sweet and choice
To him who brings it simply forth.
Do you not hate me?

QUEEN

I hate myself much more than you.
I once did hate you, envying
Your beauty, spiting all the world,
Loud as the world was in your praise,
In homage bowing low to you,
But looking at myself, the Queen,
Askance and sidelong. Oh, that roused
My blood and made it tigerish.
I did not see with my own eyes,
I did not hark with my own ear.
Mere groundless hatred saw and heard,
Ate, daydreamed, played, and slept for me.
In sadness I laid down my head,
Did what hate did. That's over now.
Hate wants to love. Love hates itself

For loving less than vehemently.
But look—here comes the youthful Prince.
Go, kiss him, call him your beloved.
Tell him I'm warmly fond of him
Despite some bitter words thrown off
In your behalf. Go, tell him so!

*(Enters the Prince.)*

PRINCE

You, lovely Queen, are whom I seek.

QUEEN

Well! Lovely? A genteel salute.
I love you, Prince, for Snowwhite's sake,
With whom you wish to be betrothed.

PRINCE

Snowwhite declines to be my bride.
She says I am of other mind
Than at the time I lifted her
Out of her shrine and brought her here.
If she is right, you are to blame.
To you I wholly give myself.

QUEEN

Whence such a feeble cast of mind
That like a wavering stalk of reed
Bends to each shaking of the wind?

PRINCE

Whence? I don't know whence, truth to tell.
But this I know only too well:
I am in love; in love with whom?
With you, who are her Grace the Queen.

QUEEN

Such love is little to my taste.
It moves too fast. Too juvenile
Your whole demeanor is for me,
Far too mercurial your mind,
Too rash such acts. Have patience, Sir,
Don't tell me of your love for me.

You have some scolding left to do
At me instead, for Snowwhite's sake,
Whom you quite callously forget.
Ho, Huntsman!

PRINCE

Who wants the villain?

QUEEN

No villain he. In hunter's garb
He is ten thousand princes worth.
Be not so rash, consider whom
Your idle storming may offend.
*(to the huntsman, who appears)*
Ah, there you are.

HUNTSMAN

At your command.

QUEEN

Act out, as if the time were now,
The scene of Snowwhite's late ordeal
Back in the forest. Here and now:
You act as if you meant to kill,
You, girl, entreat him for your life.
Your audience are the Prince and I,
We blame you if you play your parts
Too gingerly. Well, then, begin!

HUNTSMAN

Here, Snowwhite, I will take your life.

SNOWWHITE

Oh, just like that? You do not say!
Lift up the dagger first. I feel
No terror at your haughty threat.
Why would you want to choke to death
This life of mine which never has
Inflicted taunt on you or harm?

HUNTSMAN

The Queen hates you; her orders were
To kill you here, with kisses sweet
She vehemently urged me on.

QUEEN

    Ha, ha, with kisses, ha, ha, ha!

SNOWWHITE

    What seems to trouble the dear Queen?

QUEEN

    Nothing, go on. You're doing well.

PRINCE

    The villain plays the villain's part
    Most naturally; it covers him
    As snugly as his hunter's garb.

QUEEN

    Prince, Prince!

HUNTSMAN *(to Snowwhite)*

    Therefore prepare yourself for death.
    And make no difficulties, please.
    You grate like sand in the Queen's eye,
    And so must quit this goodly world.
    She who commands me wishes it.
    Get ready—why do you resist?

SNOWWHITE

    Have I no right to struggle, come,
    When rude death has me by the throat?
    Are you my death, you flinty man?
    No, no! Your gaze is mild and good,
    Upon your brow dwell gentle thoughts.
    You kill wild beasts, but no such men
    As are not openly your foes.
    I see it now—compassion makes
    Your weapon falter. Thanks, oh, thanks!
    If but the Queen were minded so.

QUEEN

    Ah, really! Was this not God's truth?
    Has what you really mean slipped out?
    In that case, Huntsman, drop the part
    So unbecoming such a man.
    Go to and charge the wicked wench
    Who frightened me all afternoon

With crafty prating, Kill her, please,
Bring here that faithless heart of hers
And lay it at your sovereign's feet.

*(The huntsman raises his dagger at Snowwhite.)*

PRINCE

What! What is . . ? Snowwhite, run away!
Villain, let go at once! O Queen,
The serpent that you really are!

QUEEN *(laughingly holding back the huntsman's arm)*

All this is but a game, you know.
Let's go into the park. Spring air,
Strolls up and down the shady lanes,
Light chatter on the graveled paths
Shall be our quarrel's happy end.
I am a serpent in your eyes,
If not much worse. No harm in that,
For the impending hour, you watch,
Will prove to you that I am not.
Snowwhite, come here. Prince, by your leave
I'm calling her child of my heart.
We were just acting, after all!
The roles were aptly cast, indeed.
In earnest, as it were, a blade
Was leveled in a hunter's hand:
"Who is the villain?"—ha, ha, ha!
Come, let us all into the park.

PRINCE

But I don't fully trust you yet.

QUEEN

Come, rabbit princelet. Huntsman, come.
Let laughter ring us on our way.

HUNTSMAN

Aye, Queen.

*(Exeunt.)*


*Change of scene. Garden, as in first scene. Enter Queen
and Snowwhite.*

QUEEN

Now you are pining, as before,
Are bitter, give me mournful looks;
Why such a wordless change of mood?
You know I do not nurse a grudge,
So you repine quite groundlessly.
The Prince has, as you surely know,
Turned back his love to you again.
You sulk, and don't remark the love
Approaching you on every side.

SNOWWHITE

Ah—the idea that grates on you
And hounds me will not leave my thoughts;
It always haunts my fearful mind,
And never, while I live and breathe,
Will I quite cleanse myself of it.
It stains my heart with tarry black
And muffles any joyous sound
Within my soul. I am so tired,
That open coffin I would seek
To lie in, an unfeeling form.
If I could just be with my dwarves
I'd be at peace, and you'd be rid of me;
I plague you, and your face proclaims
You wish me a thousand miles away.

QUEEN

No, no!

SNOWWHITE

If I could just be at the dwarves'!

QUEEN

How was it there? All still and blithe?

SNOWWHITE

Peace dwelt there, silent as the snow.
Were I with them, who were as kind
As brothers to me; in their sphere,
Sparkling with cheerful cleanliness,
Pain, like a nasty residue

Repellent to the well-bred taste,
Life's polished table never knew.
Joy, like a bed sheet, was so pure
You dropped off into sleep on it,
Into a realm of motley reveries.
Unchivalrous behavior was
Unknown among the people there.
There everyone loved gentle ways,
Conduct of breeding. Discourse sweet
Found lips that echoed in response.
Were I still there! But something drove
Me back in tears among you here,
Back to a world in which a heart
Is bound to droop and waste away.

QUEEN

There was no hatred there, you say,
Among your dwarves? Then love perhaps—
For love is fed by hate, you know,
And love above all loves to love
(You know it) frozen, bitter hate.

SNOWWHITE

I never heard an uncouth word.
Hate never troubled love. If love
Was there, I truly cannot tell.
Hatred is called for to make loving felt.
There I knew not what loving meant;
Here, where but hatred is, I know.
Longing for love as I have been,
I know of love; by hatred touched,
The questing spirit yearns for love,
While yonder at the dwarves it dwelled
In undisturbed serenity.
No more of this. It's past and gone.

QUEEN

Then let us laugh together, dear.

SNOWWHITE

No—laughing needs a different mood

From what my bosom harbors now.
I'm only in a mood to cry.
With kiss and blandishment you spurred
The huntsman, and just recently
Pricked him to murder, after all.
"Go to and charge the wicked wench,"
You said and fairly shook with rage,
Though later calling it a game.
Oh, you are full of vengefulness,
Play an unheard-of game with me,
Who know not how to guard myself.
Sink me into my grave. Her grave
Will then be Snowwhite's dear retreat.
I will attain a smiling mood
Below ground, where my joy resides.
Lay me beside it, be so kind!

QUEEN
You're smiling, laughing now, you know?

SNOWWHITE
It's for a single moment, though.
The very next retells to me
Of wickedness and woe from you,
Shakes threatening fingers, points for long,
Looks with wide-open eyes at me,
As you are doing; whispers then:
This mother is no mother, nor
The lovely world I knew—the world;
Love is suspicion, silent hate,
The Prince—a hunter; life is death.
You're not the good Queen, after all,
But the proud, sensuous one, who sent
The gory huntsman after me.
You fancy him, you flatter him,
Allow him the voluptuous kiss
By which you egg him on to kill.
I am his prey—all this is what
The other, bitter, moment says,
You'll hate me doubly now, no doubt.

QUEEN

I stoked his fire with kisses—right?
Not so? Why not speak up and tell?
Shout it out loud to the mild world,
Repeat it to the winds, the clouds,
Carve it in trees' luxuriant trunks,
Breathe it unto the gentle airs
So that with their perfume they might
Dispense it like a gift of spring.
Then everyone will sip of it,
Praise you as guiltless, call me bad,
Because I fed murder with love
And launched it with a poison kiss.
Ho, here! Where are you, Huntsman? Come.
All done with shame, kiss you I will
And call you most beloved man,
The best, most faithful, strongest, and
The loveliest and most impudent.
Snowwhite—you help me praise the man.

SNOWWHITE

Enough, enough, this maddens you.
I wish I had not touched again
That festering wound. It bleeds afresh
And now will never heal again.
If you could pardon me, O Queen.

QUEEN

To hell with pardoning, with shame,
Long-suffering, mercy! Ho there, serf!

*(Enter huntsman.)*

HUNTSMAN

You called, exalted lady?

QUEEN

My chosen man—but first the kiss.
If I could perish . . . but it seems
I am to stay and speak a while.
I must explain this game of ours,

Or she who's It will call it coarse.
Why don't *you* speak in my stead, tell
The foolish, stricken maiden here
My hate of her, my love of her.
Brandish your knife—no, don't, my dear,
Let it repose right in its sheath,
All you should do is comfort her,
Tell her of things she can believe
And I find calming; muffle all
And mute it back to what it was
Before this saucy game began.
Begin, then, and be on your guard,
Say not too little, lest your speech
In its jejuneness say too much.

HUNTSMAN

Snowwhite—come over to me, do.

SNOWWHITE

Why, gladly—since I fear no more.

HUNTSMAN

I meant to kill you, you still think?

SNOWWHITE

Yes—and yet, no. I throttle *yes*,
And *no* is quick to tell me yes.
Say that I do believe. Speak so
That *yes* must aye believe you, for
Of *no* I'm tired, and *yes* is dear.
I will believe whatever you say.
I love to say "yes, I believe."
*No's* gone against my grain so long.
So: yes, I do believe you, yes.

HUNTSMAN

This is Snowwhite's true voice, you see?
Mistrustful, she is not herself
But a tormenter who torments
Herself and others bound to her
By bonds of love. If now I call

A lie what rank suspicion says,
A barefaced, venomous lie—why, then
Snowwhite believes me—do you not?

SNOWWHITE

Yes, and how gladly! Why not yes,
Oh, yes, to anything you say.
Yes-saying feels so good, is so
Endlessly sweet. I hold it true.
Why, if you piled up fairy tales
As high as heaven, tried lies on me
Palpably crude, grossly inept,
I still would answer yes, forever yes.
Faith never has so sweetly swelled
My heart as now, nor—yes—confessing
Been half so dear as now, this *yes*.
Say what you like, I will believe.

HUNTSMAN

How easy you make things for me,
For the dear Queen, and for yourself.
For which, my thanks. Still, think, my girl,
I'm peddling shameless lies to you;
In my dear Lady's interest
I string together idle tales.

SNOWWHITE

No, no, don't lie to your own self.
I know it was your soul that spoke.
I trust you. Oh, such confidence
Walks surely, never falsely trusts.
Speak lies—my very credence will
Convert them into silver truth.
I say beforehand yes to all;
Whatever you may think and speak
My yes will stamp the truth on it.
Speak, for within my trusting mind
Is held a captive, as it were,
Who longs to leave his fusty cell.

HUNTSMAN

    Free then of guilt and shame I here
    Pronounce the Queen. You think it right?

SNOWWHITE

    I, think it right? Why, on what grounds
    Should I distrust such welcome news?
    I do believe it; carry on.
    Run on, as briskly as you like.

HUNTSMAN

    That she enflamed me to the crime
    With fiery kisses is untrue.
    The fairy tale that says so, lies.

SNOWWHITE

    How could it *be* truth when you call
    It lie. Go on, I am convinced.

HUNTSMAN

    That she detests you like an adder
    For your fresh beauty's sake, that is
    A lie. Why, is she not herself
    As splendored as a summer tree?
    Look at her now, and call her fair.

SNOWWHITE

    Fair—oh, how fair. The lavish splendor
    Of spring is not so exquisite.
    Why, her magnificence excels
    The polished marble given shape
    By an accomplished sculptor's hand.
    Sweet as a mellow dream is she,
    The fervid sleeper's fancy can't
    Imagine such a fairy shape.
    And she, they think, is envious
    Of me, who like the winter maid
    So still and cold stands by her side?
    That's past belief. How could it be?
    Continue then, you see I am
    Quite of your mind in this affair.

HUNTSMAN

    Beauty does not hate beauty so
    As fairy tales have given out.

SNOWWHITE

    No—for she is so fair herself,
    How could she hate the sister form
    Which, lying at her feet, implores
    To be permitted as her shade
    To dwell in her vicinity?

HUNTSMAN

    That I had meant to kill you is
    Of rankest childish fancy born.
    I never had the heart for it.
    Why, from the very start I felt
    Touched by the childish sweet appeal
    Which pleaded from your lips and eye.
    I lowered knife and arm as one,
    And drew you up to me, sweet maid.
    The deer which sprang across our path
    I stabbed instead. Was it not so?

SNOWWHITE

    I hardly think it worth our while
    That I should vouch for it. But, yes.
    Of course it's yes. That's right. Why, yes.

HUNTSMAN

    The Queen did not have someone sent
    Out to your dwarves to poison you.
    The poisoned apple is untrue,
    Poison the lie which so asserts.
    This venomous assertion is
    Plump and enticing like a fruit
    Swelled with seductive glamor, but
    So made inside that he who dares
    To taste of it is stricken ill.

SNOWWHITE

    A black and crazy lie, to scare
    Small children with. Throw out the lie.

What more can you bring forward? Please
Produce another silly lie
And wring its neck so deftly, do!
Why is the Queen so silent?

HUNTSMAN

She's musing over sorrow spent;
The error which possessed you two
And wrought malignant flaring strife.
So much misjudgment makes her weep.
Snowwhite, go kiss her—if I may
Make free to ask the favor now.

SNOWWHITE *(kisses the Queen)*

How pale you are! Excuse my wish
To take the life out of your pallor
With kisses. Would they might drink up
All traces of the dreary hue
Which so impairs your loveliness.
Say, Huntsman, don't you know more news?

HUNTSMAN

Oh, so much more. . . . But I fall silent now,
Ends meet with kisses now, although
The onset is not over yet.
The Queen is nodding graciously,
And in her grace my speech is quenched.
Blissful, I therefore hold my peace.

*(Enter the King, the Prince, ladies in waiting, nobles.)*

SNOWWHITE

Kind Father, press your august seal
Upon the quarrel, still unquenched,
Between two such high-flaring hearts.
Take this kiss, and as messenger
Of peace stamp out the jealous flames.

KING

I always thought you *were* at peace.
What sort of quarrel, my sweet child?

QUEEN

No quarrel left, just smiling words,

Jest which parades with serious mien
And fools you with portentous brow.
A feud there was, but is no more.
Love knew how to prevail, and hate
Went down before such force of love.
I hated, but it was in jest,
An impulse, reckoned genuine,
Though but the menace of a whim.
That's all, and now is dulcet peace.
Yes, injured envy thought a while
It had to hate. Ah, but it hurt
Myself far more than others here.
Snowwhite corroborates it all.

KING

And is this hunter free of guilt?
This Prince indicts him bitterly.

SNOWWHITE

The very sky is not more pure.
You think, perhaps, that he has had
Illicit concourse with the Queen,
Kiss and embrace exchanging—oh,
Believing that, you would mistake
This fine man's character and mind,
Which are as noble as a gem.
Love has to love him, honor crown
His brow, beyond a doubt. Brave man,
As many thanks as gratitude
May owe to you, I shall repay.
*(to the King)*
All is in harmony, my Lord,
Contention looks like skies of blue.

KING

If so, a miracle indeed
Has come to pass in this brief hour.

PRINCE

The cad is thus a cad no more.

QUEEN

    Be silent, noble Prince—ignoble
    Is your insistence on a flaw,
    Which you depict, time and again,
    And strive to make proliferate
    Instead of fade. Had it grown big,
    We would not now be standing here
    So peacefully assembled. Give your hand,
    Forget the error in a friendly clasp.

PRINCE

    Shall I forget that the accursed
    Poisonous evildoer here,
    This villain dressed in hunter's green,
    Did but a little hour ago
    Rut on the Queen's abundant grace?
    Try making me forget that I
    Am an anointed prince and lord,
    But not this sin, which is too great
    To be forgotten or annulled.

SNOWWHITE

    Come, there's no sinning any more.
    Sin fled before us and has now
    Become extinct. As faithful child,
    I kiss this sinner's hand and plead
    With her to sin a great deal more
    In such endearing way. What, Prince?
    Would you pile up contention here?
    Have you forgotten that you swore
    An oath but some few hours ago?
    Did you not pledge the Queen your love
    And bend your knees before that sight
    Of splendor, reverend and sweet?
    Now show your love, for it behooves
    You most of all, in merry mood
    To offer homage's shy kiss.
    I, too, have thought myself ill used,
    Cast out, pursued, the prey of hate.

How stubborn and obtuse I was
To think at once of wicked sin,
Adopt suspicion in such haste,
And to be blind in bitterness.
Throw off your premature ideas
Of law incensed and sentence passed.
Mildness is law here, mildness is
Peace crowned and regnant; do observe
The lovely consecrated feast
Which scatters sins high in the air
And as with petals plays with them.
Be glad you can be of good cheer.
Could I but speak the way I ought
In such a great and sacred cause!
But my persuasive gift is small,
What's more, delight's too wild in me,
I am too boisterously filled
With lofty contradictory joy.

QUEEN

  How sweetly said, you lovely child!

KING

  Accept this kiss, and all must hold
  A feast of loyal joy today.
  Prince, you are best advised to hug
  The mood of universal bliss.
  You surely would not want to be,
  Or seem, a stranger to a joy
  So heartfelt, giving, and intense?
  What? Still an angry look?

PRINCE

  Not angry, yet not reconciled;
  And at a loss for what to say,
  *(Exit.)*

QUEEN *(to Snowwhite)*

  And you? Not weary any more,
  Back in your laughing, cheerful mood,
  Scattering happiness like seeds?

SNOWWHITE

>Not weary. Never again. But look, the Prince
>Shuns our rejoicing timidly.
>Does that become a noble lord?

QUEEN

>Why, yes, it does; a coward, anyhow.

SNOWWHITE

>I don't know if he is or not.
>But this was not well done by him.
>Go, Huntsman, bring him back to us.
>*(Exit huntsman.)*
>I will berate him when he comes;
>And he is sure to: all he wants
>Is to be sedulously coaxed.

QUEEN

>Then he'll be sure to be your swain.
>And then—then I submit we should
>Remind ourselves—How shall I put—
>What do I say? Ah yes, then say,
>As by coincidence one day:
>"You goaded him with fiery kisses
>To the—"

SNOWWHITE

>Oh please be silent, please! It was
>The tale said this, not you and never I.
>I said so once, once thus—
>That is all over. Father's here,
>Accompany us all inside.

*(All walk towards the palace.)*

(1901)   Trans. W.A.

# 3 / Some Early Responses

Franz Kafka

# Letter to Director Eisner

Dear Herr Eisner,
Thank you for the package, my professional education is rather
scanty anyhow. You say Walser knows me? I don't know him. I have
read *Jakob von Gunten*—a good book. I haven't read the other books,
for which you are partly to blame since, in spite of my advice, you
did not want to buy *The Tanner Siblings*. Simon is, I think, a character in that book. Doesn't he run around everywhere, up to his ears
in happiness, and in the end nothing comes of him except that he
provides amusement to the reader? That is a very poor career, but
only a poor career gives the world the light that an imperfect but
pretty good writer wants to generate—at all costs, unfortunately.
Viewed superficially, of course, such people are running around
everywhere; I could list a few of them for you, myself among them,
but they are distinguished by nothing but that lighting effect in
fairly good novels. One might say that they are people who were
somewhat slower at emerging from the last generation than others;
you cannot demand that all people should follow the regular leaps
of time with equally regular leaps of their own. But the laggard in a
march never catches up with the rest of the marching column. The
step left behind soon acquires such an appearance that you would be
willing to wager it is not a human step, but you would lose the
wager. Consider that the view from a racing horse on the track—if
you can keep your eyes on it—the view from a horse leaping the
hurdle, say, certainly shows you the utmost presence, the veritable
essence of racing. The unity of the stands, the unity of the living
spectators, the unity of the surrounding region at that certain time
of year, etc., even the last waltz of the orchestra and the way people
like to play it nowadays. But if my horse turns back and won't take
the jump and shuns the hurdle or runs off and disports inside the
arena, or even throws me, naturally the total view will seemingly
have gained a great deal. There are gaps among the spectators; some
fly, others fall, hands wave back and forth as though responding to

From Franz Kafka, *Letters to Friends, Family, and Editors*, trans. Richard and Clara
Winston (New York: Schocken, 1977), 60–61.

every possible wind, a rain of fleeting interrelationships falls upon me, and it is quite possible that some spectators feel it and concur with me while I lie on the grass like a worm. Would that prove anything? [fragmentary]

(Prague, probably 1909)

Robert Musil

# The *Stories* of Robert Walser

[*Geschichten* (1914)]

These thirty little stories will seem overly playful to people with a practical bent and to women with strongly charitable inclinations. These people will accuse the stories of lacking character, of being quirky, of flirting with life, perhaps even of being heartless and of letting themselves be impressed by the bewildering determination with which insignificant things, say a bench in the garden, fill out their place in the world. In sum, although people will not actually say so, it seems to me that what will irritate them deep down is that these stories lack ethical depth. But that's how it is: our emotional responses toward many objects are so well established that we treat our reactions as if they were inherent in the objects themselves. We can consider a large fire in a theater—a case that brings us to Walser[1]—only as a terrible misfortune. Someone could perceive it as a splendid or well-deserved misfortune: since we are liberal minded, we naturally do not wish to prevent that person from doing so; but we do feel entitled to demand reasons. If he has absolutely no need of reasons but considers it all to be simply as delightful a misfortune as we consider it horrible, then we suggest first the following approach: must be depraved; if all we find is an endearing chap, then we say that he is lacking in ethical depth or that he sins against the seriousness appropriate to his subject matter. Indeed, it is not only on sad occasions that we demand this respect towards subject matter, we also ask for a certain sobriety in pleasure. A writer must speak with such delight about the greenness of the meadow that we feel how—in a flash—his very heart is turning green. Or, suppose he says he cannot bring himself to do so and that, far from being green, the meadow is an economic disaster since factory workers cannot eat meat due to the beautiful meadows of the agriculturists. If all he feels is that the meadow is just plain dumb green and good only for boules—and this is no doubt the simplest thing one would want to say about a beautiful expanse of grass—then we would probably tend to feel that the emotional demands of a meadow are somehow being treated negligently. Now, as it happens, far from having the remotest intention of setting himself up as a revolutionary or of putting himself beyond the emotional pale, in most of his responses Walser is a charming, hearty, somewhat fantastical fellow. One, however, who constantly sins against the inalienable aspiration of objects without and within—that we accept them as real. To him a meadow is now a real object, but a moment later only something on paper. Whenever he daydreams or gets angry, he never loses the awareness that he is doing so in writing and that his feelings are all wired up. He can suddenly tell his figures to keep quiet, letting the story speak as if it were a figure. Shades of puppetry, Romantic irony; but in this fun there is something else, reminding us from a distance of Morgenstern's poems— all of a sudden the gravity of real conditions begins to drizzle along the thread of a verbal association. Except that in Walser's case this association is never purely verbal, but always works on the level of meaning. As a result, the line of feeling he happens to be following rises as if for a great movement, then pulls away, and, satisfied, goes jauntily on towards the next enticement. I by no means wish to claim that there is not some playacting involved. In spite of the extraordinary verbal command, with which one could become infatuated, this prose is by no means a belletristic playacting, but rather a human one, with much softness, reverie, freedom, and the moral affluence of one of those seemingly useless, lazy days when our most steadfast convictions ease into a pleasant indifference.

Franz Kafka: It seems to me nevertheless that Walser's specialty ought to remain as much and that it is not a suitable foundation for a literary genre. My discomfort with Kafka's first book *Meditation* [*Betrachtung*] is that it seems like a special case of the Walser type, although it appeared earlier than the latter's *Stories* [*Geschichten*]. Here also we find contemplation in a form for which fifty years ago a writer would surely have found the title "Soap Bubbles"; it is enough to refer to specific distinctions and to say that here [in Kafka] the same manner of invention sounds as sad as the melody there [in Walser] was gay: there, something freshly baroque; here, in intentionally page-filling sentences, something of the conscientious melancholia with which an ice skater executes his long curves and figures. Here also there is very great artistic control over oneself; perhaps only here do these little endlessnesses waft over into the void, a humbly chosen nothingness, a friendly softness, as in the hours between a suicide's decision and his act—or whatever one wishes to call this feeling, which can be described in various ways, since it only resonates very faintly as a dark overtone; and very delightful it is, only too indistinct and faint.

[Musil subsequently discusses Kafka's story, "The Stoker."]

(1914)   Trans. M.H.

Walter Benjamin

# Robert Walser

There is a lot of Robert Walser to read, but there is nothing written
about him. What can those who know how to take these market-
place glosses in the right spirit tell us: those, that is, who, unlike the
schmuck trying to exalt them as he "elevates" them to his level, can
glean purifying vigor from Walser's insolently unassuming avail-
ability. Few, indeed, realize what this "short form," as Alfred Polgar
called it, is all about; how many hopeful butterflies find refuge in its
modest chalices from the cliff face of so-called great literature. And
the others have no idea how much, amid the sterile jungle of the
newspapers, they owe the gentle or prickly blossoms of a Polgar, a
Hessel, a Walser.[1] They would even think of Robert Walser last. For
the first stirrings of their miserably bookish education, which is all
they have in literary matters, prompts them to emphasize "cultivated" and "noble" forms as a means of recouping what they call
the nothingness of the content. And just then in Walser they notice
a going to seed which is very unusual and difficult to describe. In
any contemplation of Walser's pieces what is most crucial is the insight that this nothingness is weighty, this letting go a form of
perseverance.

It is not easy. While we are used to seeing the mysteries of style
emerge out of more or less fully developed and purposeful works of
art, here we are faced with language running wild in a manner that
is totally unintentional, or at least seems so, and yet that we find
attractive and compelling. A letting go, moreover, that ranges
through all forms from the graceful to the bitter. Seemingly unintentional, we have just said. Occasionally there have been argu-
ments over whether that is really so. But, the moment we recall
Walser's admission that he never corrected a line of his things, we
realize that it is a mute argument. There is no need to take him at his
word, but it would be worthwhile to do so. For then the following
thought can put us at ease: to write and never to correct what one
has written amounts certainly to a total merging of extreme lack of
intention with the highest form of intention. So far, so good. It
need after all hardly prevent us from getting to the bottom of this

running wild which, as we have already said, takes every form. To which we now add: with a single exception. Precisely that of the most common form for which only content is crucial, and nothing else. Since the how of his work is of such moment to Walser, everything he wishes to say takes second place behind the significance of the actual writing itself. We are almost tempted to say that the what dissipates in the writing. This needs some explanation. And here we stumble across something very Swiss in this poet: reticence. There is a story about Arnold Böcklin, his son Carlo, and Gottfried Keller:[2] One day they were sitting in an inn as was their wont. The reserved and taciturn ways of the drinking partners had made their table famous. Once again the company was sitting together in silence. After a long time had elapsed, the young Böcklin observed: "It's hot"; then, a quarter of an hour later, the elder one added: "And absolutely calm." Keller for his part waited some time, then got up saying: "I'm not drinking with such babblers." This peasant reticence with words, captured here by a witty bon mot, is Walser's turf. No sooner has he taken up his pen than he is overpowered by the urges of a desperado. Everything seems lost; a surge of words gushes forth in which each sentence only has the task of obliterating the previous one. In a virtuoso piece he turns the following [Schiller] monologue into prose: "Through this sunken path must he come." He begins with the classical words: "Through this sunken path," but then anxiety catches hold of his Tell, and seeing himself already defenseless, small, and lost, he continues: "Through this sunken path, I believe, he must come."

There have certainly been precedents. This chaste and artful clumsiness in all spheres of language is a legacy of the fool. If Polonius, that archetype of babblers, is a juggler, Walser wreathes himself Bacchus-like with garlands of language which keep tripping him up. The garland is indeed a figure for his sentences. But, like the heroes of Walser's prose, the thought staggering about in them is a thief, a vagabond, a genius. Indeed he can only portray "heroes," cannot get away from his main figures, and letting matters rest with his three early novels, has henceforth devoted himself solely and uniquely to the brotherhood of his hundred favorite vagabonds.

It is well known that in Germanic literatures there are above all some great exemplars of the windbag, lazybones, and petty thief of a hero who has gone to the dogs. A master of such figures, Knut Hamsun, has just recently been celebrated.[3] Eichendorff,[4] with his

*Taugenichts* (Good for Nothing), and Hebel,[5] who created Zundelfrieder, are others. How do Walser's figures make out in this company? And where do they come from? We know where the *Taugenichts* comes from. From the forests and valleys of Romantic Germany. Zundelfrieder, from the rebellious, enlightened lower-middle class of Rhenish towns at the turn of the century. Hamsun's figures from the primeval world of the fjords—they are people whose homesickness draws them to the trolls. Walser's? Perhaps from the Glarn Mountains? Or from his native Alpine meadows at Appenzell? Not in the least. They come out of the night, where it is darkest, a Venetian night, one might say, lit by skimpy lanterns of hope, with some festive cheer in the eyes, but troubled and sad to the point of tears. What they cry is prose. For sobbing is the melody of Walser's loquacity. It divulges where his loves come from. From madness, that is, and from nowhere else. These are figures who have put madness behind them and can thus remain so laceratingly, inhumanly, and unfailingly superficial. If we wish to find one word to describe what is pleasing and uncanny about them, we may say: *they are all cured.* We, of course, never find out about this process of healing, unless, that is, we dare approach his *Snowwhite*—one of the most profound compositions in recent literature—which itself alone would suffice to explain why this seemingly most playful of all writers was a favorite author of the unrelenting Franz Kafka.

The wholly exceptional gentleness of these stories is apparent to all. But not everyone sees that the life they contain is not the nervous tension of decadence, but the pure and lively atmosphere of convalescence. "What horrifies me is the thought that I might be successful in this world," as Walser puts it in a paraphrase of Franz Moor's dialogue. All his heroes share this horror. But why? Certainly not out of any aversion to the world, nor out of moralistic resentment or pathos, but for purely epicurean reasons. They want to be able to take pleasure in themselves. And they are quite exceptionally adept at that. They also display an unusual nobility in this regard. And have an unusually strong right to do so. For nobody enjoys as does the convalescent. Everything orgiastic is alien to him: he hears in brooks the flowing of his replenished blood and, blowing from the tree tops, the purer breath on his lips. Walser's people share this childlike nobility with the figures of fairy tales who, of course, also arise from night and madness, in other words from myth. It is usually assumed that this awakening took place in the established religions. If this is the case, then the form it took was

at least not simple and clear cut. To find that form one has to explore the great secular confrontation with myth which the fairy tale
represents. Of course its figures do not simply resemble Walser's.
They still struggle to free themselves from suffering. Walser begins
where the fairy tales leave off. "And if they have not died, then they
live to this day." Walser shows *how* they live. His pieces, and here I
wish to end as he begins, are called: stories, essays, poems, short
prose, and the like.

(1929)   Trans. M.H.

# 4 / Recent Essays

Elias Canetti

# Robert Walser

Robert Walser's special characteristic as a writer is that he never formulates his motives. He is the most camouflaged of all writers.
Things always go well for him, everything constantly delights him.
But his enthusiasm is cold, since it leaves out one part of himself,
and that is why it is sinister. For him, everything turns into external
nature, and the essential thing about it, its innermost being, fear, is
something he denies all his life.

It was only later that the voices crystallized, getting back at him
for all the concealment.

His work is an unflagging attempt at hushing his fear. He escapes
everywhere before too much fear gathers in him (his wandering
life), and, to save himself, he often changes into something subser-
vient and small. His deep and instinctive distaste for everything
"lofty," for everything that has rank and privilege, makes him an
essential writer of our time, which is choking on power. One hesi-
tates to call him a "great" writer according to the normal usage,
nothing is so repugnant to him as "greatness." It is only the brilliance of greatness to which he submits, and not its demand. His
pleasure is to contemplate the brilliance without taking part in it.
One cannot read him without being ashamed of everything that was
important to one in external life, and thus he is a peculiar saint, not
one according to outmoded and deflated prescriptions.

His experience with the "struggle for existence" takes him into
the only sphere where that struggle no longer exists, the madhouse,
the monastery of modern times.

Every writer who has made a name for himself and asserts that
name knows quite well that for this reason he is no longer a writer,
for he administers positions like any burgher. But he has known
people who were so utterly and purely writers that they just couldn't
be successful at it. They wind up extinguished and suffocated, and

From Elias Canetti, *The Human Province*, trans. Joachim Neugroschel (New York:
Continuum, 1978), 228–30.

have the choice of burdening others as beggars or living in a mad-house. The writer who asserts himself, who knows they were purer than he, can't endure having them around for long, but he is quite prepared to venerate them in the asylum. They are his split-off wounds and keep vegetating as such. It is exalting to contemplate and get to know the wounds so long as one does not have to feel them in oneself anymore.

The torment of success: it is always taken away from others, and it is only the unsuspecting, the limited, those who do not tell them-selves that there were better people than they among the robbed, who are able to enjoy success.

The prestige that writers draw from their martyrs: from Höl-derlin, Kleist, Walser. Thus with all their claim to freedom, vast-ness, and inventive-ness, they merely form a sect.

I am tired of riding the high horse of this artistic pretense. I am not yet even a human being.

"I can breathe only in the lower regions." This statement by Robert Walser would be the watchword of writers. But the courtiers do not utter it, and those who have won fame no longer dare even to think it. "Couldn't you forget about being famous for a while?" he said to Hofmannsthal, and no one more forcefully characterized the em-barrassing thing about the upper orders.

I wonder whether there is, among those who build their leisurely, secure, linear academic lives on the life of a writer who dwelled in poverty and despair even *one* who is ashamed.

Martin Walser

# Unrelenting Style

Shall we enroll our author forever among the ranks of the so-called controversials? We know that is no longer necessary. Those who understand have compared him with Shakespeare, Mozart, Schubert. That he is a classic is admitted today even by those who do not much care for him. Especially by them, perhaps. So they can be rid of him. Apparently there is no need to fear that anyone will actually read him. From the man who did the very fine translation of *Jakob von Gunten* into English, I learned in 1973 that in the previous year sixteen copies had been sold in the United States of America. Ten years ago I would have said zealously: And how many hundreds of thousands of Hesse! But I don't say that any more. Years of associating with Robert Walser's books have developed in me a sensation that might be captured like this: There are books that spread like brush fire, and books that sink gradually into us; they never cease sinking into us, and we never cease wondering that books can have such an endless, gentle weight or that there are in us such depths to be awakened. The accompanying feeling is something like happiness. I have now had this experience three times: with Hölderlin, with Kafka, and with Robert Walser. For an author who offers such a degree of inexhaustibility, there is no need to fear, for all eternity. So one is free to just talk about him. If one can.

I would like to talk about the tone of Robert Walser. Who would not be glad to help free this author from the scented cloud, still with us, of the gifted dilettante, that of the charming genius living entirely off soulful spontaneity? The big-shot critics and colleagues, those especially, recognized in him the most charming of all authors. Since they believed him nothing more than that, they were only too glad to consider him a kind of exquisitely lyrical poet-simpleton, who had staggered out of the competitive arena and whom they might readily grant a grain or two of their superior attention. I would like to mention the manufacturedness of Walser's tone—his attempt to treat life ever more exclusively as if it were writing. With the counterbalancing smile that for him had to accompany every big word, he himself designates what he has thus achieved as his "unrelenting style."[1]

When his first book, *Fritz Kochers Aufsätze*, appeared in November 1904, one reviewer believed the author to be an overrefined offshoot of some extremely refined house; possibly even of Mann's *Tonio Kröger*, which had appeared the year before. But even if one did not take the contents to be pure realism—"Papa has carriages and horses," and such like—the Fritz Kocher tone sounded overdelicate and graceful. And naïve. Incredibly naïve. Well, at least Tonio Kröger had never been that, not for one second. How haughtily Tonio Kröger despises everything that is not up to his current standards! And with what naïve vehemence Fritz Kocher adores everything that happens to come before his scent-addicted nose! That is how literary society perceived and maintained the author: as the Paragon of Sincerity, the poet who walks about on dreamed legs, and who, to his good fortune, does not quite know what is happening when yet another pretty line springs forth from him. In brief appearances in the Wedekind salon in Munich, involving dreamily sudden passes at girls' legs and chitchat as easily confiding as it was productively uninhibited, Robert Walser was only too glad to play the role of boy-page-cherub-poet against a completely provincial Alemannic backdrop. Even more so from 1905 to 1912, amongst the twining *Jugendstil* tendrils in the western suburbs of Berlin, which seemed as though prepared for him alone. For a time, he played the shepherd boy, the Beardsley figure from Biel, so well apparently that for years afterwards he was forced to hear that he was really much better in person than on the page. The split began when they all thought him nothing more than his role. In the eleven or twelve or thirteen hundred prose pieces that he wrote because he considered himself "bottomlessly unsuccessful" as a novelist, he was forced to react again and again to the period from 1895 to 1913. In 1928, when even his prose piece writing had been soured for him by the general lack of recognition, he described his debut in literary society with *Fritz Kocher* in the prose piece "The First Step" ("Der erste Schritt"): "So-and-so-many years ago I sped, not unlike a traveling journeyman, through brownish green forests and over shimmering, yellowish blue flowered, unforeboding plains, and arrived in all innocence at a place where important contemporaries, standing one and all on a terrace, received me with a friendly smile, crying out with unmistakable amusement: Behold, here marches and dances our way one who still seems completely unassailed, unspoiled."[2] He says that fellow writers to whom he himself had told his life story would then thunder at him regularly: "How gloriously embarrassed you then stood there, so magnificently sweet natured, with such a wonderful shepherd-boyishness?"[3] And in 1932, shortly before he had to quit, he wrote in the prose piece "The Midget" ("Der Knirps"), this too is one of his roles: "Now and then, his facility, arising as it were from a kind of sleep, bore the stamp of calculated naïveté or artificial artlessness."[4]

The grotesque thing is that his cleverest contemporaries—including even Kafka and Walter Benjamin—were unable to see through the shepherd boy, whereas he himself, the naïve child, was able to formulate grandiose diagnoses of this misunderstanding in terms as clear and hard as a diamond. As well intentioned as Kafka and Benjamin were towards Robert Walser, I nevertheless believe that Kafka's much-cited love for him is a creation of Max Brod, who, in his capacity as editor, published Robert Walser's prose pieces for years, and also, by a stroke of intellectual luck, attempted just about the only analysis of his poetic method we have. Walter Benjamin, with his admiring murmurs about the enigmatic qualities of Robert Walser's "language returned to the wild" and his "letting himself go," did more to nourish the cultural rumor of the naïve poet than to make his poetics comprehensible.[5]

There is a fine touch of lunacy to Robert Walser's finding himself surrounded by "younger intellectualizers" in the late twenties who urge him, as he himself puts it, to "free [himself] from his novice ways," while also making him "most respectfully, i.e., painstakingly, aware of the jewel of still being absolutely unaccomplished."[6]

So who is naïve? Those who took him (and still take him) to be a *Jugendstil* version of the Romantic *Taugenichts*, or the Walser who could describe his role so accurately:

They laugh at me primarily because I seem in earnest. They think it happens unwittingly, whereas in fact it's by design. But my vocation, my mission, consists mainly in making every effort to keep my audience believing that I am truly simple. I give them the illusion that unspoiledness and naïveté still exist.[7]

If he shows himself at his "full height, carefully gone to seed from head to toes," then, he says, "this sloppiness [is] a product of art."[8] Even Walter Benjamin was unequal to this sophistication from the town of Biel. Possibly he got his impressions from reading magazines now and again. The reader who can survey the *Collected Works* has an easier time recognizing the author as an author.

Today anyone can see, for example, that the *Kocher* prose piece about poverty cannot have been written either by a scion of affluence or by somebody who is totally naïve. In one of his favorite roles, that of the servant Tobold, Walser reworked his stay at Dambrau Castle in Silesia in the fall of 1905; in the guise of Tobold he lets himself say that he wants to take part always in the battle of good against evil, of the "movable ones against the hard boiled . . . , of the diligent toilers against those who do nothing and nevertheless still stay on top, in the battle of the innocent against the shrewd and the sly." [9] In this Robert Walser battle plan, the front which pits the movable against the hard boiled tells us most about the struggles of his life. Mobility, getting carried away, instability are his wealth and his poverty, his happiness and his distress, the sine qua non of his existence, which he assumes and develops as his profession. He wants to become an author immediately, of course. And famous, with all his heart. Fritz Kocher is already the fundamental figure for his life: The child, a poet; or, the poet as child. And he enters with just as great a thirst for great enterprises as Hölderlin at his youngest. "I am frightfully ambitious," says Fritz Kocher. [10] Like the earliest Hölderlin, he feels almost naked with ambition. He has no theme, he just wants to write. But was he really so themeless, so pointlessly and emptily ambitious as he, the scruple-struck lad from the petite bourgeoisie, accuses himself of being? The manner in which this child Fritz Kocher turned away from the industry of his home town! He does not concern himself, he says, with what is made in the factories. "I only know that all the poor people work in the factory, perhaps as a punishment for being so poor." [11]

The poor are punished for being poor "by having to work in the factory"; in other words, it serves them right. Since Swift made his famous "modest proposal" that the poor should sell their extra children to the rich for the Sunday dinner table, thus simultaneously solving the problems of a surplus of children and a shortage of suckling pigs, probably no ironic author has gone as far as our young naïf, who declares poverty a crime properly punishable with work in a factory. I find it astonishing how soon he completely masters the art of pronouncing an evil reasonable. And in the next few years, this becomes the task through which he develops his style. Personal distress, far from being represented or lamented as such, is to be answered experimentally in the affirmative, and this yea-saying to want and distress is to be developed ever more reasonably, ever more richly. He dispatches Fritz Kocher off into the forest to this end. Subsequent Robert Walser characters also find in nature an otherness which has at least the advantage of not being a society intent upon doing harm. It is as with Hölderlin. Thus nature is not a fixed opposite, but is itself a process. "The forest flows," we read in *Kocher*, "it is a green, deep flowing away, a running away, its branches are its waves."[12] In this movement, which of course proceeded from the ego and was amplified by the forest, the ego itself is caught up, unstable as it is. Whoever flees society and comes suffering into the forest, will experience, in this region of amplification, a back and forth with nature that finally makes him able to say his happiness kisses his suffering, indeed his suffering is his happiness; he has learned that from the forest. Happiness and suffering are the closest of friends. Here it sounds precocious, cheeky, preposterous: At the end of the forest piece, which is the end of the *Kocher* book, the author can already demonstrate his kind of tone and procedure—that is, his method—applied to his own writing. He would really have preferred to pour out his feelings in front of the beauties of nature, he says, but there he learned that "pouring out in the art of writing demands a perpetual self-restraint."[13] What this colorfully spoken but still very green poet-youth formulates here might readily remind one of Jean Paul at his most mature— who would not become one of our young man's favorite authors until years later. Irony, said Jean Paul, requires "a perpetual keeping to oneself or objectification . . . [a] countering frost in the language."[14] A fellow wants to pour out his feeling, but notes it would carry him away too far, so he restrains himself and instead formulates a completely different tone so as not to lose himself; when he hears how the countertone sounds, compared to the spontaneous one, he is pleased. We can see that the countertone stems from a countersteering. Instead of letting go, a person has oppressed himself a little. And lo and behold, he has a much clearer sense of himself as his own oppressor than he would have as one who gets carried away and loses himself. That too is an achievement; it reminds one of the rewards for good behavior in a petit bourgeois childhood and adolescence. Instead of biting into the chocolate, one makes a face as if one had bitten into it. And this becomes a method. It is decisive that no blows from the world around him—and these blows, as we know, get lower and lower—could make this author give up writing.

Goethe, I believe, once advised his colleague Eckermann that young writers should be careful not to get caught up in projects that would more or less tie them up for a long time. He himself, said

Goethe, could have achieved still more if he had been less intent on long-term projects and had thus been even more alive to the stimulus of the moment. It took the crashing failure of Walser's three novels, written and published in Berlin, and the know-it-all advisors drawn like bluebottles to this failure, to drive Walser away from the novel and make him a writer of short prose, at the mercy of everyday events. That is, he had to be driven in a great fall from his planned course, in which he competed with Cervantes, Stendhal, Dostoyevsky, and Keller, down to the chicken-run of the manufacturer of prose pieces, who could answer to his experiences only with the kind of complaisance and limited scope grimly prescribed by the fine arts page. In 1907 he could still write, rather breezily, to Christian Morgenstern that he would rather join the army than become a supplier to magazines. Yet that is exactly what he became. He put up with it until 1933. But by then, in the prose piece form allotted him, he had truly carried out his project. Even if one wants to gnash one's teeth a little in rage, reading his *Robber* novel, at the thought that more of the kind has been lost to us, Walser's enforced concentration on the prose piece bore an uncanny fruit: a life-novel, consisting of a thousand and several hundred segments. In the late twenties he himself wrote that in his opinion his prose pieces formed "nothing more nor less than parts of a long, plotless, realistic story. For me the sketches are . . . shorter or lengthier chapters of a novel. The novel, on which I am constantly writing, is still the same one, and it might be described as a variously sliced-up or torn-apart book of myself." [15]

He had his ego appear in this book in the roles of the youths Fritz, Wenzel, Simon, Kasimir, Fridolin, Felix; in the bookkeepers Tanner, Helbling, and Josef Marti; in the servants Tobold and Jakob; in those eerie celebrities named Mehlmann, Oskar, Wladimir, and Schwendimann; he was also fond of letting himself be guessed or even easily discovered as Kleist or Brentano; naturally he also wrote about Kleist, Lenau, Lenz, Cézanne, Watteau, Mozart, Beardsley, Voltaire, and so on, without bringing in himself every time as the main character. But he liked to dress up as [Schiller's] Karl and Franz Moor; even more, in the garb of the Prodigal Son. And best of all, and more and more frequently, with no name at all. To him, names were things that tied up, pasted down, shut in. He was much fonder of appearing under labels signifying a function, an activity, a relationship; most preferably as a child; then as a page; as a servant. In a prose piece from the late twenties about a lackey, his gift for mobility dictated the following to him: "He lacked the desire to be what he was."[16]

If one wants to get any real sense of Walser's style—without getting lost in a merry-go-round of aesthetic ghosts—then at some point one must also take into account that possibly no poet has ever wanted to make a friendlier entrance into the world. Whenever he recalls it, one senses this. "Certainly I was beautiful then, I know that now," he says.[17] Everything made him glad, he said. He loved everything, welcomed everything without exception. "Yes, I used to stand and go about like a person entitled to say he was carousing." "The wind flew in blue waves across the field, and bells chimed, and everything was namelessly beautiful . . . , I was free as never before . . . , each thought a part of life, and each living apparition immediately a thought." And he needed no objects for his rapture. "The simple awareness of existence, enchanting me, dug down deep within me in search of love, which was flying through screens and walls all about into the Measureless and whatever came next. Outside, amid the echoes and the noise, a stillness embraced me as though I could never again fail. Everything around me was blue as fluttering flags and red as blossoming lips and young as the eyes and cheeks of children. Then seriousness was alongside laughter, and dying was alongside living. So it went, back and forth in constant movement; the flashing days were like shimmering fruit." Naturally, he then took a man on the road at night to be Jesus Christ. Naturally, for him writing and praying were one. But the seraphic tone of the man from Biel produced a dissonant echo in his time and world. And he does not reject this echo, but absorbs it and makes it his own. He says, quite right. Not immediately. Not all at once. It's not that easy to say yes to the world's saying no. After the fall, being the fallen one, he first had to feel himself all over. When he fell in Berlin with his novels, he wrote his first Brentano prose piece.[18] It says: "He saw no more future before him . . . , the past was like . . . something incomprehensible. All justifications scattered like dust. Voyages and journeys . . . had become oddly repulsive to him: he was afraid to take a step, and at the idea of changing his abode he shuddered as at something monstrous." First he begins to reproach mankind, then himself: he was "the most unreliable, most lascivious, and least faithful thing on earth." At this point one sees directly how it is possible for the world, for society, to arouse someone dangerously against himself. He would like to separate himself from the person who put him in this situation. He still believes in a better self within him. "O, his person," he cries, "he would have liked to rip it away from his essence, which was still good. To kill one half of himself so as to save the other from destruction, to save the man from destruction, to keep the God within him from being completely lost." Then he returns to Biel. Beaten, but sheltered again. His prose piece "The Entrance" ("Die Einfahrt") may very possibly be the most insuperably beautiful piece ever bestowed upon a country by a returning Prodigal Son.[19] "Slowly, as if it were prey to a profound reflectiveness, and as if it had a need to advance hesitantly, the train moved along; it was a workman's train." "The homeland, and the high, golden thought of it, soared around my heart . . . O what beautiful train riding among mild-mannered, sensible, serious fellow countrymen, all the way into embracedness." By virtue of the powerful gratitude of one who has been saved—or who considers himself saved—all the prose pieces about the return home are simply magnificent. In Biel, to be sure, he was not forced to perform the self-alienating salon tricks of Berlin; for here he remained from the outset at his own level; but the lack of confirmation and recognition, the not being perceived or understood, broke him down again over the years until, in the end, he was worse off than after the Berlin fiasco. Now there was no longer any Switzerland to shelter him. At this point something occurred that he, who had called himself "a man of development,"[20] had feared—life itself threatened to grind to a halt. A prose piece that bears witness to this after six years of Biel is called "The Street" ("Die Strasse") (1919):[21] "I had taken steps that had proved useless, and now I went into the street, upset, numbed. First I was as if blind, and thought no one saw anyone any more, that all had gone blind, and that life had come to a standstill because everything was groping about madly." This is also the night he goes up to a figure standing in the dark. But it is no longer Jesus Christ, as in bygone days. Now he says: "This heaped-up collectivity wants and does nothing. They are tangled in one another; they do not move, are as if locked in; surrender themselves to indistinct force, and yet are themselves the power that weights them down and fetters their minds and limbs." He escapes to Bern. Wants to stay in motion. But by failing utterly to perceive his movements, the world around him intensifies its negation of them. He must not only cope with this. He must—unrelentingly—approve it. To sanctify the misery by lamenting it in the tone it had itself set, that was out of the question. A professional does not permit himself such directness. He could not allow himself to be an unjustly unrecognized writer and complain of it into the bargain. No, he cries: Nothing does a writer such good as a hefty portion of nonrecognition. Nothing is as good as misery, because from the vantage point of the worst you can only look ahead to better. "Stendhal was well off because he was badly off." [22] That's how the unrelenting style puts it. It is a movement of existence that allows not a single second of peace or safety. Recognition is, after all, as the story "The Negro" ("Der Neger") puts it, "a soft shattering of something that, supported by unconsciousness, has been building within us." That is unrelentingly petit bourgeois realistic. Every one of Walser's readers knows his racing fugues of modesty, those orgies of belittlement that eliminate all imitators as surely as do Kafka's subjunctive snares. Yet in Robert Walser, as in Kafka, there is nothing that expresses solely the author and not his fellow citizen just as well. Not for one second did Walser feel justified as an author. No experience can extinguish his passionate desire to be the good neighbor. Nor can experience diminish the strength of his love. But as a result of all that experience, love gradually begins to consider itself comic. He has his "Robber" go to a doctor and say: "maybe my illness, if I can call my condition that, is that of loving too much. I have a horrifyingly large fund of love in me, and each time I go out on the street I start to love something, someone, and everywhere as a result they call me a man of no character: I would like to request you to laugh a little at that." [23] Max Rychner, who could not have known this passage, compared him to Shakespeare; after which Walser—in his own tone—called himself the Shakespeare of the "wee prose piece." So the blissful early tone has evidently attended the school of hard knocks that inclines one to comedy. After the "midsummer night's dream," the person in question knows that under certain conditions love is comic; indeed—if it does not behave correctly—it can even be called a sickness.

In other words, the blissful tone, which has never been at all naïve, produces a terrible echo, which the author does not bewail, but instead prefers to amplify to the shrillest. "If dying must be done anyway, I'd sooner die willingly than unwillingly"—that is what his style dictates. [24] Anyone who still takes the passage in the "Negro" story about recognition as demolition to be the product of a genius feigning modesty can be directed to passages of the same tendency that have no aesthetic horizons, but only moral ones. For instance in 1926: "Admiration, after all, begets arrogance, hardness." [25] Or, both morally and aesthetically, in 1915–16: "Isn't defeat better than the wan smile of triumph?"[26] And again from the twenties, in a section in which he again represents himself as a forty-year-old child: "Mockery and lovelessness made him happy."[27] And in the Wladimir role: "Seemingly peculiar that he admits having often been joyous as a down-and-out and morose as a success story."[28] The worst is really and truly the best—that is the thrust in the development of his unrelenting tone; it is to be demonstrated again and again until calm plausibility sets in. In a prose piece written after 1930, he still allows himself to be questioned about his failure; letting himself respond, we read, "reluctantly and at the same time openheartedly." So, just as in Kocher's days, self-restraint and pouring out belong together. And that is how the answer turns out: "Bad writers [he said] are sometimes more entitled than good ones. . . . Anyway, all recognition has forever tended to turn into a trap or a ditch, and lying within rejection are all kinds of encouragement."[29] In the prose role of the adventurer, he uttered the same with shrill pride: "I would wither away, lose myself, if everyone with reason to do so were to respect me."[30] Here he ascribes to contempt rights that are downright fabulous. One must often recall as the source of energy the petit bourgeois Christian treasure chest of morality; otherwise this radical cultivation simply evaporates into aesthetics. In one of his finest roles, that of the servant Tobold, he says: "if, of my own free will, borne by courage and compassion into higher frames of mind, I renounce heaven: then will I not, sooner or later, as a reward for upright behavior, fly to a heaven many times more beautiful?"[31] One should also place the instability of his ego, and thus his mobility and preference for change, within their real context, which he himself names often enough—poverty: "only the poor man is able to walk away contemptuously from the narrow self, so as to lose himself in something better, . . . in movement that does not come to a halt, . . . in the vibrating generality, in the inextinguishable mutuality that bears us" (1919).[32] Or: "There was a cheerful mobility and freedom in poverty. The cold provided scorching heat."[33] A poor man, we read somewhere else, respects everything except himself. "Where would he have gotten respect for himself?"[34] Indeed, perhaps he even began writing, he says, because he had been poor and needed to start a sideline to make himself feel richer.

I have spent too long showing his method only as it applies to himself; it is really one-sided to demonstrate the elaboration of his unrelenting irony only through the ever-more-successful touting and justification of his own failure. His dialectical art, derived from the most personal experience of deprivation, can also solve problems. He proves this as early as *Jakob von Gunten* when, in a crazy passage of dialectic, we are led to concede that only the suppression of freedom makes it possible to experience freedom, that only a life not being lived is really a life.[35] Twenty years after *Gunten* he still calls his "never having lived" a "gigantic, magnificent, radiantly green tree."[36] The cunning of reason which Hegel discerned in world history is not for one second alien to this author's perception of reality. "The bad are of use to the good,"[37] he says. "The Swiss," he writes twenty years after *Gunten*, "perhaps owe their freedom not only to William Tell, the fighter for freedom, but also to Governor Gessler, who considered freedom out of place, and who provided the former with the occasion to set himself in motion. . . . The shover and the shovee, the one who exerts pressure and the one who shakes it off, somehow complement each other; and as for freedom, it desperately needs governors, etc., in order to grow."[38] Later on, he presents Tell and Gessler as "a single contradictory personality."[39] What interests him is solely the "circumstance of the giving-cause-for-movement."[40] Tell and Gessler are an "inseparable unity;"[41] for him movement becomes the highest value, as for Hölderlin, Fichte, Hegel, and Kierkegaard it had become the highest value, the only absolute. "The movable is always the most just," he writes.[42] One can now look back differently on his preference for misfortune, on his serious attempt to praise his failure, on his preference for the negative, on his ability, developed to the point of virtuosity, to experience, represent, and acclaim as the most pleasant that which is least pleasant: Nothing should remain, absolutely nothing. Thus whoever spent a moment among the elect would the very next moment have to face becoming one of the disadvantaged. The orderly, the diligent, the much approved, the good, the successful, the ruling, the fortunate, the living: because time continually pulls all things down, everything will be thrust next moment into its opposite. That is all they have to look forward to now. "Because things cannot be otherwise than that they become otherwise, they became otherwise," says he in jest, in a truly Hegelian mood.[43] On the other hand, whoever exists only in the negated moment is constantly looking forward to existence. Maturity was always alien to him. Spring engendered autumn in him, and autumn spring. There was no summer. Absolutely not to be in the present

moment, or perhaps to be absolutely not in the present moment—
therein lies the countertone that he developed against time as well as
world.

Once we have followed Walser all the way into these frequencies
of his realistic sense of history, we can finally get beyond compassion for the author as one who was and still is misunderstood.
Otherwise it would be like feeling sorry for Jesus because he was
crucified. Some people are simply able to transform what has been
inflicted upon them into their work. They become objective. That
is the highest goal. Robert Walser achieved it. And formulated it
thus: "My activity is stronger than I."[44] There is—one must say this
with all due awe—no one whom Robert Walser approached more
often or more boldly than Jesus, whom he simply called his favorite. As early as 1913 the man who had returned completely beaten
from Berlin to Biel allowed himself the perspectival luxury of calling himself a "vanquisher," whereupon he of course immediately
had "an attack of laughter."[45] If one entrusts Jesus' message of love
to the unrelenting style of this terrible, gentle man from Biel, it
comes out like this: "There is something almost malicious in not
hating anything."[46] Or: "With modesty you can practically do in
somebody."[47] And can any author formulate more like Jesus than one
who writes that his best lines are those that "make the reader consider
himself superior to the author?"[48] People have restricted themselves
too emphatically to extolling this author's funny-masochistic lapdog
antics as the droll achievement of his charm. Someday we must realize that he mediates himself into Jesus just as exactly and uninhibit-
edly as he did into Kleist, Brentano, Schwendimann, or Knirps. He
has the scribes thus confront his favorite role, Jesus: "Your modesty
is all artfulness."[49] As with the Negro role, this applies at least as
much to the Bieler as to the Nazarene. He can now express everything, even the greatest bliss, in the form of a negation. He can also
express the worst in the form of a completely perceptible, magnificent affirmation. At times one can even get the impression that the
style has reached these turning points all by itself. It has become
that highly developed; an author's existence has become that profes-
sionalized. But however monstrous its achieved phrasings, this stylistic movement borrows not a gram of weight from any traditional
workshop for making impressions. While playing, he achieves sentences such as the following: "It will sound exquisite if I say I know,
with enviable precision, that the present essay contains errors, and
that this certainty is something beautiful."[50] Such a sentence has an

effect on me like news from a better world. Just when, by dint of interference, scolding, disdain, and rejection, they have almost wholly deprived a man of his sense of self, he manages to make the bundle of impositions his own and uses it to produce phrases of Mozartian lightness. That his most extreme gestures should still be light as a feather is probably due to the way his Alemannic mother tongue watches over these unrelenting movements. This linguistic womb pursues her child, who wants to become pathetically independent in standard German, with all kinds of ridicule. Often enough one watches Robert Walser hammer the most intractable raw materials of the thing-addicted Alemannic dialect into a lyrical sketch that is fine to the point of making one faint.

If I now go on to point out that agglomerated contradictions begin to proliferate almost frighteningly in his works, I should add—as stridently as possible—that these knots of contradictions, through which he practically allows his prose to decompose itself, have nothing in common with the mania for opposites that led a different "literary often-mentioned" of the age to set up mechanically opposing rows of dummy concepts, between which the author dashes back and forth for a while, only to betray them cheerfully to one another, while raising himself above them to hover on high, untouchable, most eminent, and incontestably himself. It does make a difference whether one descends from Friedrich von Schlegel or from Hegel. Schlegel prided himself on his ability always to top one heaven with yet another. Robert Walser wanted to learn to renounce heaven completely, so as to become worthy of an even higher heaven, which he would then, of course, also renounce for a still higher one. In reality, that meant renunciation of heaven, absolutely; but not as a single act—rather, as a lifelong movement in the work. Hence the conspicuous increase in his style of compound contradictions: He would have preferred most of all to hyphenate each adjective with the opposite that language holds in store. And he does that, too, more and more frequently. Just as Kafka, with his chains of speculations, gradually throttles all movement by his characters so that absolute indeterminacy can assume its dominion in prose, Robert Walser takes each point wanting to pin itself down and jams it headlong into its counterpoint, thus yielding a knot of words that shivers with the tension of contradiction; or perhaps a patch of bright darkness such as one finds in Rembrandt—one can no longer dwell anywhere. Gradually one does grasp that the language arisen from our story of pain always arose through a tearing apart of something whole. Because of its origins, language is always a specialized deprivation. It is language because of its ability to distinguish life from death. In reality, faith and skepticism, life and death, and so on are unstoppable points along paths of movement; it is only when the various verbal labels are superimposed that they are transformed into opposites, in a way that annihilates their movement, and therefore their sense. The last step of this prose restores the real contradictions as inducements to movement. Nothing is separated from anything any more. Everything is linked by its negation to everything else. In a century in which authors have adopted the oddly unprofessional notion of considering themselves the representatives and vicars of all that is possible, we would be almost morally endangered if this genius of change had not arisen among us as a corrective. His countertext earns us a future: "To a great degree, one possesses only what one lacks, for then one must seek it." [51] Has the negative ever been as beautiful in anyone else's writing? To me, some of his sentences seem suitable as an elegiac apocalypse of the bourgeois age.

Having failed to reach their goal, the benefactors could no longer sleep in peace. [52] If *everything* can be expressed as deprivation, then language has for once exhausted its possibilities. After all, that is the purpose for which language arose in the first place. Robert Walser makes no reproaches—he loves, and loves, and loves again. So he arrives as if by himself at his unrelenting mildness: "The vouchsafers are out in search of supplicants." [53] This is Jesus, despecialized. The last days of a class that set out alongside the declaration of human rights. But something must have then gone wrong. Maybe domination. Once again, domination. Once again, humanity—well not quite. But the apocalyptic mildness of that sentence stores and preserves completely the splendid first steps of this class: "The vouchsafers are out in search of supplicants." I want to bring one final sentence of his into play; I have already marveled at it a hundred times, and each time it has rewarded me. It arose out of the author's experience, out of his utterly clear recognition that he was born to mediate and that mediation is work that does not survive the second in which it is accomplished. The sentence comes from his prose piece "Sketch" ("Skizze"): [54] "The garden somewhat resembled a thought fortunately never thought to a conclusion; and my sketch I compare—although I have no idea where I get the effrontery to do so—to a swan, singing with unheard-of ardor, who gives voice screechingly to unmediated things." So, with the simplicity of a

Hölderlin and the beauty of a Robert Walser, he expresses his work as a writer. The fact that he compares his activity, which is stronger than he, to a swan giving voice screechingly to unmediated things tells me how wrong it was earlier to suggest that there are those who can simply fashion what has been inflicted upon them into their own work. I wanted to redeem our author from the fate of having to be pitied. But that emphasis underlines the notion that the prose piece just completed can affect his consciousness retroactively and stabilize it for what is to come. This is precisely not the case. The distress, which individual prose pieces mediate, passed away with them. The author then had to confront the next imposition without any particular stability. If I say that, through his assent, he succeeded in conquering all adversities, then, just like those who thought the Kocher boy merely naïve, I have been taken in by his irony. Perhaps, at times, even the author himself fell for his own unrelenting, stronger-than-he-was form of writing. True irony always wants to be involuntary.

The sketch that screeches about unmediated things makes me realize that with this author one can never reach solid ground. He himself never reached it. The sketch screeches out loudly and beautifully that the poet's business of mediation never achieves permanent success. Writing means to make necessities look like freedom. But the *like* remains a *like*, and needs to be sung and screeched with ardor. Let us briefly recall that Robert Walser by no means undertook to mediate everything. He had a deadly serious precondition for creativity: Freedom from other work. His being dismissed so often as a clerk in Zurich attests that, in order to write, he always first had to make his "out-of-the-way thoughts" come true.[55] Only when "occupied to the highest degree" at "being unoccupied" could he write.[56] At such moments he had the heat turned off, "for I didn't want to have it easy, I wanted to freeze."[57] Here we find him already in the midst of mediation. To be free, however, in the sense of unoccupied, was his axiom, so to speak. All distress occurring thereafter he accepted as a task, and began to rewrite it unrelentingly into something beautiful, something right, something welcome. If I'm to die, then better willingly. But mediating, after all, means to create not another condition, but only a different consciousness about the same condition. For Robert Walser the situation is no different than for Fichte, who was, as it were, unable to derive a single second of truly stable self-awareness from his lifelong "I–not I" billiards—and thus had to keep on playing a lifelong game with the theory of science. For Robert Walser it is no different than for Kierkegaard, who could not for a single day call off the dialectical hunt in which skepticism roused faith out of the bushes and faith in turn roused skepticism; otherwise his existence would grind to a halt and become undetectable. So too it may have been with the other saints of movement: Saint Hegel, Saint Marx. So it was, as has been noted often enough, with Kafka, the only ironist in the German language comparable to Robert Walser.

Irony leads to nothing. The unrelenting hunt itself is the only bearable situation, a situation comprised of nothing but movement. And this movement supplies the sensibility with a sound that can be experienced—an almost perceptible rustle of identity. If the unrelenting dialectical hunt were to come to a stop, so would life; one would get lost in the disequilibrium of distress. So long as it is possible to rewrite every incoming grain of distress into a grain of freedom—that is, to mediate it for consciousness as the sweetest, most welcome of experiences—then the movement may continue; one can believe in equilibrium, can almost hear the yearned-for rustle of identity. But if one is then put against one's will into an asylum, the mediation, the writing itself, is no longer possible. There is no irony that could transform this asylum into a freely chosen home. Freedom, the precondition for writing, is totally absent.

Don Quixote has to surrender. His only name now, it turns out, is Cervantes, or Robert Walser. He is no longer a boy, or a page, or a servant, or a lackey, or Jesus, or a child—in other words not an author, either. Only a quite healthy man of fifty-five, one who can defend himself no longer and, from now on, for another twenty-three years, will make no attempt to defend himself—i.e., to write. Truly, to welcome this inmate's existence, with unrelenting irony, as a fate imbued with freedom—to do that, a person would really have to be sick. But since he is healthy, he lets the asylum be an asylum, lets himself be a patient. The swan becomes an inmate, and screeches about unmediated things no more, enduring them instead, silently, it seems, and probably also patiently. His twenty-three-year-long silence denies us any right to speculate. But if you please—we can be truly happy with what the swan from Biel gave us, while still a swan.

(1978)  Trans. J. McC.

Tamara S. Evans

# "Am awake and lie yet in deep sleep": Robert Walser and Modern Perception

A young writer, a contemporary of ours, travels to Berlin where he meets Robert Walser and his publisher friend Paul Cassirer. All three get into the gondola of a hot air balloon, ready to fly to Königsberg on the Baltic Coast. They have taken along a few bottles of wine—red and white—and some delicacies that Walser had received from Mrs. Mermet, his good friend in the Swiss Jura. Once all the ballast has been thrown overboard, they take off on their journey, rising higher and higher, vanishing from the earth. This is the time to discuss business with one's publisher; and later, while the young author writes postcards to friends, Walser composes a long letter addressed to Frieda Mermet, thanking her for the delectable food and ensuring future supplies. At daybreak, they watch the carrier pigeons disappear in the distance.

Despite its seeming defiance of facts, this anecdote embedded in an homage to Robert Walser conveys a glorious insight, for it captures in an ingenious way some of the most characteristic aspects of Walser's style in life as well as in literature. Like so many works of Walser, it blends the real with the unreal: Walser and Cassirer did fly in a balloon to the Baltic Coast in 1908; Walser did receive food packages from Mrs. Mermet—but not until they had become friends sometime after his return to Switzerland in 1913. On this dream journey Walser is portrayed adrift in the air and yet with both feet on the ground: Unlike Schiller's poet in "Die Teilung der Erde," who was dreaming when the earth was divided up and everybody rushed to secure a piece for himself, our traveler is not altogether in the clouds. Food and drink have been taken along; business is not being ignored; and the thank-you note is by no means oblivious to future needs. Like Walser, E. Y. Meyer—the young Swiss author who devised this journey on the occasion of Robert Walser's one-hundredth birthday in 1978—has transmuted time into space: his trip to Berlin takes them back to the Königsberg of Kant and the eighteenth century.[1] Finally, like Walser, the author debunks conventional concepts of reality; he juggles with the hypothetical in a manner that is as serious as it is jocular: we laugh, but we also question our perception of time and space as separate categories.

In a book by another contemporary writer, we find the following anecdote:

> Somebody tells a true story of a meeting between Lenin and the poet Robert Walser in the Spiegelgasse in Zurich in 1917. Robert Walser asked Lenin only a single question: "Do you also enjoy eating this Glarner Birnbrot"? I do not doubt the authenticity of this anecdote even in my dreams, and wake defending Robert Walser. I am still defending him as I shave.

Once again, the inventor of this reportedly "true story"—Max Frisch in his *Sketchbook, 1966–1971*—has captured the Walseresque with uncanny accuracy; once again we are led into a world between truth and untruth.[2] For Walser and Lenin did indeed live at that address, although during different periods. Walser's question is absurd when we consider first of all that it is Lenin whom he is asking for such trite information, and secondly, that it is 1917, the year of the Russian Revolution, with Lenin just about to leave Zurich to return from exile. In Max Frisch's dream Walser does not care to ask the predictable or expected question; he will not allow himself to be manipulated into a political discussion and maintains a standpoint that is disengaged and entirely ahistorical. Like his fictional character Jakob von Gunten, the fictional Walser is shown to have "the courage to be the person he is."[3] Reason enough for the inventor of this "true story" to continue defending Walser after he awakens.

The relatively recent rediscovery of Robert Walser owes a great deal to writers like Max Frisch and E. Y. Meyer. Both tell us—even though in a whimsical way—that Walser must be taken seriously; for placing Walser in the illustrious company of Kant or Lenin neither diminishes nor ridicules him. In the case of E. Y. Meyer, both Kant and Walser stood godfather to his artistic development. Frisch's defense of Walser implies that Walser's stubborn rejection of convention together with his courage to be himself, may be potentially as subversive as Lenin's commitment to "new methods of putting humanity in order," to borrow from Walser's own words on Lenin in "A Slap in the Face et cetera."[4] And when Frisch, a few years later, listed Walser among those authors who have had a lasting influence upon him, it is because Walser's writings show no trace of an "a priori reconciliation with his country's history as well as its present."[5]

If Walser is to be taken seriously nowadays, it is not only because he turns out to affect our contemporary generation of readers. The term *rediscovery* suggests that Walser was considered innovative and revolutionary in his own period. Although never belonging to a school or movement, Walser was part of the avant-garde of his time. "Modern writers," Irving Howe writes in *Decline of the New*, "find that they begin to work at a moment when the culture is marked by a prevalent style of perception and feeling; and their modernity consists in a revolt against this prevalent style, an unyielding rage against the official order."[6] Like other early-twentieth-century artists and writers, Walser, too, searched for new forms that would adequately express a radically altered perception of the world. In the following pages I will look more closely at some aspects in Walser's work that express his modern awareness of the diffraction of reality. To strengthen my case, I will establish links between Walser and some of his better-known contemporaries in literature as well as in the other arts.

"Am awake and lie yet in deep sleep"—I have chosen as title and motto for our exploration this line from an unpublished poem (1925) because it directs us to one of the preferred places from which Walser and his fictional characters perceive the world.[7] Asleep while awake, awake while asleep: because of this simultaneity and congruence of seemingly opposite states of awareness, Walser is both the inhabitant and the creator of a world no camera can focus upon, a world in which the invisible can be seen next to the visible. Walser's world, like that of Jakob von Gunten who can never quite decide whether he is awake or dreaming, is—to use Jochen Greven's phrase—a "world-in-between," "eine Zwischenwelt."[8]

Frequently, often within the flow of a single sentence, without clear demarcation, Walser's landscapes turn into dreamscapes. In *Der Räuber-Roman*, a novel with a highly fragmented narrative structure which Walser wrote in the midtwenties and which was not published until 1972, the first-person narrator tells the following episode from the protagonist's past:

I am irresponsibly forgetful. Once, you see, in a pale November forest, after he had visited a printer's shop and chatted with the proprietor for an hour or so, the Robber encountered the Henri Rousseau–woman, dressed entirely in brown. He stopped in front of her—stunned.[9]

In this passage Walser is referring most likely to a canvas by Rousseau, entitled *Walk in the Forest* (ca. 1886), portraying in the left middle-ground a lady dressed in brown, with piercing black eyes that Walser will mention later on.[10] The Henri Rousseau–woman is one of those "Figuren auf Pump," a figure on loan, whose sudden appearance, according to Theodore Ziolkowski, triggers amusement as well as shock; these two reactions help not only to create an atmosphere of the phantastic but also an awareness of the brittleness of fictional reality, which in an uncanny way points to the brittleness of reality in general.[11] As the lady in brown is strolling along the woodland path with the Robber and engaging him in a challenging conversation about his way of life at the periphery of society, one wonders whether she has stepped out of the painting to join the Robber in what on the narrative level represents the real world, or whether he has stepped into Rousseau's forest of Saint-Germain. Whatever the answer, the Robber's adventure points to an affinity between Walser and Henri Rousseau whose naïveté, based like Walser's on conscious artistic volition, goes hand in hand with his rejection of conventionally perceived reality. They share in their separate media the suspension of "rational expectations," the blending of dream and reality, and "[the telescoping] of different moments in time."[12] Rousseau and Walser anticipate the Surrealists' belief in the "resolution of the states of dream and reality—in appearance so contradictory—in a sort of absolute reality," as André Breton was to put it in his first Surrealist manifesto of 1924.[13]

Equivalents of Walser's *Zwischenwelten* can be detected in the works of one of the most creative and independent representatives of modernism, namely Paul Klee, who had been suggested as an illustrator for one of the earliest editions of Walser's poetry, and to whom—if only in passing—he has been compared by a number of critics. In a conversation with a colleague at the Bauhaus, Klee called the world he represented in his paintings "eine Zwischenwelt," which he defined as follows:

I call it a world-in-between because I feel it in between the worlds externally perceptible to our senses and because I can receive it inside me in such a way as to be able to project it outwardly in correspondences. The children, the insane, and the primitive still or once again have the capacity to look there.[14]

Klee's strange, primordial creatures in paintings such as *Magic Theater, Raggedy Ghost,* or *Earth Witch* belong in that world-in-between as do some of the figures that Walser's characters, who fade in and out of varied states of consciousness, come up against at all hours of the day. In his 1917 story "The Walk," the grotesque lunch with the most hospitable Frau Aebi is the stuff of nightmares. As the meal progresses, Frau Aebi gradually turns into a veritable she-demon, demanding the narrator's full obedience in exchange for a good meal. Although fully alert, he is like someone struggling to awaken from a terrible dream, force-fed against his protests, "almost suffocating and . . . already perspiring with terror."[15] The encounter in "The Walk" with the giant Tomzack, the uprooted and homeless creature, is Walser's lurid projection of his own untamed state in the world and thus the counterpart to the scene with Frau Aebi. Tomzack, half human being, half monster, whom the narrator meets on his stroll through town, is not of this world, for in his eyes there is "a glare of grief in overworlds and underworlds" (p. 70). Frau Aebi as well as the giant are creatures in the manner of Klee; they are "things that go bump in the night": projections of childhood fantasies, projections of deep-seated anxieties.

To praise the child, the insane, and the primitive as did Klee, the Futurists, and implicitly Walser himself, and to assume such a precognitive point of view for one's own artistic creations implies rebellion—a revolt against academicism and the classical canon of beauty dictating harmony and good taste. Klee wrote in his diary: "I am starting to learn all over again: I begin to execute forms as if I knew nothing about painting."[16] According to Pierre Reverdy, Picasso called upon himself "to learn everything, that is to say to begin everything afresh."[17] André Gide had advocated in *Les Nourritures terrestres* (1897), a book that was to influence an entire generation of artists and writers, to forget everything one had ever learned from books; he considered this *désinstruction* to be the true beginning of all education.[18] Walser, too, conveys the impression of starting from scratch: in his first book, *Fritz Kochers Aufsätze* (1906), a collection of school compositions, and in some of his utterly simple, early poems ("A Little Landscape"—1898; "And Went"—1899; see part 2 of this volume) that have freed themselves of *Jugendstil* ornamentation.[19] Werner Hofmann has pointed out that the artists who at the beginning of the twentieth century left behind the easily flowing linearity of art nouveau set out for the desert in search of new unusual formal experiences; Walser's Jakob von Gunten, too, takes off for the desert—quite literally, in order "to escape . . . forever, or at least for a very long time, from what people call European culture" (p. 153).[20]

Jakob von Gunten's escape into the desert is tantamount to an exodus from historical time; small wonder that he and his former history teacher had never managed to get along (p. 59f.). Walser's perception of time is ahistorical; time is no longer "an objective, causal progression" from past to present to future "with clearly marked-out differences between periods."[21] He shares with his contemporaries a revolt against nineteenth-century historicism and the repudiation of memory "in so far as it is organized logical conservation of past experiences."[22] In Walser's first novel, *Geschwister Tanner*, Kaspar, the brother of the protagonist and a painter, wonders what the point would be of going to Italy to improve his painting by learning from the past. Simon tears up his childhood memories because they are useless, and in his speech to the innkeeper at the end of the novel he admits to be stepping carelessly on his memories in order to run all the more freely. Josef Marti in *Der Gehülfe*, Walser's second novel, destroys the diary he has started to write, and Jakob von Gunten is virtually incapable of putting together his résumé. When after several failed attempts he finally does manage to hand in the account of his life, it defies average expectations altogether. Instead of writing when and where he was born, he states: "born on such and such a day, raised in such and such a place" (p. 59). For the most part, the account is kept in the present tense: it conveys what Jakob is or hopes to become. Although called "A Diary," *Jakob von Gunten* leaves the reader at a loss as to when the individual entries were made and as to how much time has elapsed from one entry to the next. With the demise of the time structure characteristic of diary keeping, *Jakob von Gunten* becomes in a very real sense a *journal intime,* not registering the objective and measurable process of time but mapping the explorations by way of dreams and day dreams into the inner chambers of Jakob's own self and of the few he really cares about.

Jakob von Gunten perceives time in spatial terms, as a mosaic design of sorts. Thus he exclaims in his dream at the end of the novel: "How peculiar that was. The particular weeks eyed one another like small glittering gems" (p. 153). Susan Sontag's recent observation that Walser "spent much of his life obsessively turning time into space" is apt.[23] As Walser put it himself in "The Walk," he is not interested in journeys; what he is engaged in is a "fine circular stroll," a walk, in other words, that takes him back to where he started; thus time, too, is transmuted into a two-dimensional geometric shape.

The perception not only of time but also of the objects surrounding an artist who is "awake and yet in deep sleep" signals a break with the past. From Walser's particular perspective it is possible to see through things and to perceive what they normally conceal.[24]

Kant had argued that the objects we behold and the meanings we affix to them depend on the position of the viewer. But not until the late nineteenth or early twentieth century did the awareness of the relativity of the phenomenal world become endemic. In an essay on Franz Stuck, who "learned to see naïvely" and who taught both Klee and Kandinsky in Munich at the turn of the century, Hugo von Hofmannsthal notes that to the eyes of a child or an artist "a helmet might as well be a flower pot . . . and a goblet can be taken for a hollow pineapple open at the top or a fat gleaming snake's head." Hoffmannsthal concludes that "by stripping forms of their banal meaning, the artist has once again become a mythmaker in the midst of chaotic reality."[25] Since the basic form or *Gestalt* is transposable, the content of what we perceive becomes variable. In some of Klee's late drawings, the forms of angels and devils are barely distinguishable from one another. He would also paint the same subject twice: once as *Hat, Lady, and Small Table* and once as *Lady Demon*. Similarly, but in fact long before Klee or Giorgio de Chirico for that matter, who stated that every object has two appearances, "one the current one, which we nearly always see and that is seen by people in general; the other, a spectral or metaphysical appearance beheld only by some rare individuals in moments of clairvoyance and metaphysical abstraction,"[26] Walser, too, was aware that the same form does not mean the same thing at all times. To Joseph Marti in *Der Gehülfe*, Mrs. Tobler suddenly appears as a mermaid emerging from the sea; the hospitable and horrible Frau Aebi of Walser has a place both in time and in myth. If the protagonist in Robert Musil's *Young Törless* sees objects, events, and people in two different guises, so, too, does Jakob von Gunten. Kraus, his best friend at the institute, exists not only in the here and now but also as Joseph in Egypt: "The times of Abraham come to life again in the face of my fellow pupil." When Potiphar's wife tries to seduce Joseph, "then Kraus, I mean Joseph, refuses. But it could very well be Kraus, because there is something very like Joseph in Egypt about him" (p. 82).

In contrast to the nineteenth-century viewer, his twentieth-century counterpart has ceased to be autonomous beyond all doubt. Objects begin to emancipate themselves from the subject who categorizes them. Theo Elm, in an essay on Peter Handke, remarks that modern literature alienates *transcendental* reality, which consists of objects and our a priori cognition of these objects. Instead, modern literature with its awareness of our limited and hence limiting cognition attempts to represent—albeit in approximations—*transcendent* reality; this is the thing in itself, beyond the way in which we have traditionally viewed it and beyond our normal understanding of it.[27] Thus, the things we normally perceive around us in stasis begin to act independent of our volition. Examples can be found in Döblin, Kafka, Musil, and Rilke. In Walser's work descriptions of such experiences are legion. In *Der Gehülfe*, Mr. Tobler's absurd and doomed inventions—an advertising clock and a vending machine selling ammunition—keep beckoning to Joseph Marti in an irritated yet pleading manner. Trees keep an eye on what Simon Tanner and his brother are up to. In Simon's account of springtime in the countryside, with nature "stretching, bending, rearing, and nearly dying from so much blossoming," Walser conveys to us a perception of a world that seems intact, yet bears the signs of future disintegration.[28] In "Welt," a prose piece written in 1902, mountains are heaving up and down, trees are flying through space like giant birds, buildings bump into each other like drunkards. Taking mercy on the helter skelter world, God stuffs this chaos into a bag to let it dissolve into nothingness. In "Die Stadt," written in 1914, pale houses stare at the visitor with displeasure, and windows keep grimacing. Not only has the town become a wasteland, a lugubrious replica of what it once was, the universe, too, is out of joint. In a variation to the Grandmother's tale in Georg Büchner's *Woyzeck*, Walser pursues the thought of a cosmic fraud to its worst possible consequence: gone are the stars, gone is the moon, gone is the sun; all stellar and planetary points of orientation have vanished.

Walser also describes states of mind taking on shape and becoming active agents. In *Der Gehülfe* the anxiety haunting various members of the Tobler household taps quietly at the window panes, lifts up curtains to peer into the living quarters, and keeps standing in doorways to remind everyone passing by of the feeling of precariousness. By literally turning a character inside out, Walser has moods and emotions act from the outside on the person who generated them in the first place. When Mr. Tobler hears from his attorney that his bankruptcy can no longer be averted, he is thrown on a chair, "as if tons had crashed down on him, as if fists were pressing upon him, as if weights were lying on his neck, live weights, swaying, ringing, and pushing in sudden violent anger."[29] In passages like these, Walser anticipates some of the techniques used by the Expressionists. The bank teller's encounter with death sitting in a bare tree in Georg Kaiser's play *From Morning till Midnight* (1916) comes to mind; or the factory worker's eye-witness account of the explosion in *Gas* (1918), which appears to him as a fiery, contorted cat, hissing and bounding through the air; or scenes from Fritz Lang's *Metropolis* in which the subterranean monster machine, a symbol of the horrors of technology and industrialization, swallows up an entire shift of workers. While it would be preposterous to link Walser with the Expressionists' missionary zeal, the visible manifestations of anxiety and terror are portrayed by Walser with the hyperagitated plasticity that a decade later would become the hallmark of Expressionism.

Joseph Marti in *Der Gehülfe* says at one point: "All kinds of things are possible in this world if you take the time and the care to think about them for awhile."[30] Once the relativity of reality, "the present as hypothesis," as Musil put it in *The Man Without Qualities*, has been accepted, the artistic imagination can freely create visions of what might have taken place instead of what in fact did take place—of what there might be rather than of what there is. "In its present form it is not the only world possible," Paul Klee stated in his lecture "On Modern Art" delivered in Jena in 1924; thus he had no "desire to show man as he is but only as he might be."[31] In Kafka's story "Up in the Gallery," the account of what really happened in the circus is preceded by a grueling vision, written entirely in the subjunctive, of the consumptive circus rider being driven around for ever and ever. Walser, too, plays with the hypothetical. In his novels, passages in the subjunctive can run on for pages. Simon Tanner, for instance, savors every charming little detail of a possible life in a small town, possibly being married to a nice girl from a nice family—knowing all along without a trace of regret that he is not really cut out for such a life. Joseph Marti is thoroughly aware that Mrs. Tobler's trip and her leave-taking at the drab railroad station represent "all in all a picture of the twentieth century"; but for a moment her departure becomes the most dignified medieval ritual with pages and knights in attendance. Somersaulting in and out of the hypothetical, Walser debunks some of the plots of classical literature: Schiller's *Kabale und Liebe* need not have been a tragedy. "It is possible," as Walser writes in one of his microscripts, "that Louise could have acted more smartly. Probably, even most likely, I would have agreed to become the lady's maid in attendance. After all, it would not have had to be forever."[32] In Walser's prose piece "Ibsens Nora oder die Rösti," Nora too need not necessarily have slammed the door behind her, walking out of her marriage the way she did. Helmer might just as well have called her back and suggested she fix him hashed potatoes, *Rösti*, instead. If Walser's Nora is content in the end, it is simply "because Helmer had said something unexpected."[33]

Walser's whimsical play with the possible, his *Möglichkeitsdenken*, has not remained without echo if we think of the suggestion in one of Peter Bichsel's *Kindergeschichten* that America does not exist in spite of what everybody has been telling him; or of Max Frisch's portraying William Tell as a provincial reactionary rather than the idealistic freedom fighter we know from Schiller's treatment of the legend; and since time equals space, why not fly with Walser to Kant's Königsberg? Walser's ventures into the realm of the hypothetical confront the reader with a counterreality that provides not only for a "change of air," but also, and more importantly, for a change of viewpoint.[34]

How modern is Robert Walser? To be sure, Walser was far less willing than many other early-twentieth-century artists and writers to expound on his aesthetics; the examples I have chosen, however, represent a few points of entry into a work that is modernist in its perception of the world. Walser's modernism is one of a kind: while we find in his work traces of many major artistic movements following the turn of the century, the blending is uniquely his. Unpredictable, surprising, even irritating, Walser is also enchanting to those who care to embark on a balloon voyage with him.

George Avery

# A Writer's Cache: Robert Walser's Prose Microscripts

Early in 1913 Walser left Berlin, the unchallenged capital of German literature, persuaded that he had failed as a novelist. The decision to leave Berlin was probably as fateful for Walser's literary fortunes as it was necessary and inevitable for his equanimity and self-esteem. Ironically enough, the subsequent narrowing of Walser's reputation is most evident from the beginning of the twenties on, coinciding with the artistically successful attempt to broaden the scope of his writing after moving to Bern in 1921. Only *Die Rose*, a collection of "difficult" prose, appeared in the twenties—in Germany. Walser's last novel, *The Robber*, was consigned to the authorial limbo of the microscripts,[1] the much-corrected versions of prose, verse, and dialogs composed by Walser in a minuscule script in the years 1924–31 from which he made clean copies of work submitted for publication.

Walser's reasons for composing in microscript can only be surmised. Hypersensitivity to criticism, complaints from readers of his work in newspaper feuilletons about the "nonsense," the rejection of submissions by previous outlets for his writing, and the repeated failure of plans for book publication certainly affected Walser. His reclusive, solitary life centered on and had its raison d'être in writing; the microscripts were the personal repository of a corpus of writing based on self-revelation; an exaggerated sense of Swiss frugality evidently played a role. Literary factors, together with practicality, were more relevant considerations. Walser had always composed rapidly and generally made few revisions in his clean copies. Microscript facilitated spontaneity at a time when his prodigious output argued for something like a stenographic method. Ultimately, Walser's creative impulse was probably decisive. The example of two other reclusive, obsessive writers of this century, Joyce and Proust, both of whom wrote hard-to-decipher hands, both of whom added voluminously to the texts of their masterpieces when they received page proofs, make the form Walser gave his passion for expression a less peculiar idiosyncrasy.

The discussion below is based on texts selected from the earliest grouping of the microscripts, those written on high-gloss paper and presumed to have been written between 1924–25 and 26,[2] the single most productive period in Walser's career.[3] They share with the published novels Walser's hallmark of narrative immediacy, but they show him at a more advanced, still more precarious stage of artistic development than does the published work of the period. As such they deepen our understanding of Walser the man and the artist.

The overall quality of the microscripts in question is not as high as that of his published prose. The emphasis on spontaneity, the exploratory variations in the treatment of a theme in adjoining microscript texts, and the more frequent use of allusions results in many finger exercises and a good number of texts that miss the typically ambiguous closure Walser seeks. The majority of texts, however, successfully aspire to elicit aesthetic and intellectual response, whether enjoyment, identification, annoyance, or reflexion. More clearly than in the published prose, Walser is motivated by the coincidence of the need to write marketable material conforming to his reputation for diverting, humorous prose and the increasing weight he accorded to what he thought of as unprepossessing art, a theme in his writing affected by disaffection with the Swiss cultural establishment and self-styled intellectuals. The chronicle of a Bernese citizen-artist in the midtwenties still fits the characterization Walser wrote in "Eine Art Erzählung."[4] But the prose microscripts undertake more assertively to deconstruct the conventions of literature in the service of a literature incorporating the recognition that "we are all proud and we are all in some way humiliated" (193/ii) in an age that has come to mistrust "the expansive, recapitulative registers" in prose since "we are all, in fact, so shaken by the collapsing of everything great" (503/i).[5] This contrastive enterprise is broadened by variegated fields of contrasts, such as the use of a remarkably resourceful comic mode to oppose literature's exploitation of experience with authenticity of being, an irrepressible creative drive at odds with an unrequited civic sensibility, the opposition between the strictures and self-certitude in Switzerland's social and artistic life, and the risk attendant on writing in response to what one microscript calls "the figure of naked imagination" (258/iv).

If there is a single common element in the variety of microscripts, it is the omnipresent narrator as practicing writer. Whether chronicling and justifying "an everyday story," committing to paper something "journalistic," introducing a work he expects the reader will find "a horrible story," reworking material from his reading, alternately promising to write only original material, or as one of an antic array of personae, the narrator is the focal point and the controlling medium of his productions—works characterized in one text as "still another of these powerful-trivial novels that are my specialty" (266/ii).

The narrator-author characterizes divergent aspects of himself, in radically disparate fashion, that run from the self-congratulatory to putative demonstrations of incompetence. One text opens promising "once again, a marvelously lovely story" (245/iv); another describes the devices used to enliven the story as a demonstration that "I know my business, don't I?" He points to the "doubtless charming lines" (251/i) written, marvels at his forthrightness: "Splendid, the way I concede that" (260/iii), or praises his phrasing: "You agree, don't you, again that's stated with uncommon aptness and reasonably perceived" (270/ii). In the same tone, the narrator often lays claim to elegance in the work, say in a figure "of inexpressible elegance" (260/i), in the elegance of the language, the setting of the story, or even the elegance with which a lawbreaker was executed (261/iv).

Other texts claim much less command of the writer's craft. Midway in a comic love story on a Dubois and a Figurina, the narrator observes: "Odd, how confused, how thicketly entangled I'm narrating here" (480b/v). After particularizing the effect of separation on a female beloved, the narrator says of the statement that he really is not certain "whether that is just a trite phrase or pondered poetic prose proven by proofs" (193/ii). Nominal incompetence and uncertainty can be more self-incriminating. The climactic sentence in a "decidedly old-fashioned" love story describes conflicting impulses following the first embrace of socially and temperamentally distant lovers. While the narrator allows that his sentence may indeed measure up as art, he nevertheless advises the reader: "Better you don't examine this sentence" (188/iii). In an avowedly comic morality, retold for "uplift of the soul and warning to the same" (259/i), a working-class girl who sports antique rings acquired at auctions expects the well-to-do dandy who takes her riding in his car will marry her. The narrator's disbelief mounts at each repetition of the notion until disconcerting himself: "the gentleman will be contemplating further auto trips along with shovings in, I'm losing the thread and you, you gaze at me." Feigned-real uncertainty is underlined in the prelude to a plot-laden "criminalistic story" where the muse answers the narrator's appeal for support with: "What is it this time?" (186/i). Further into the text, uncertain about plot details, the narrator cites a voice calling to him: "It's about time you free yourself from all those banal stupidities." The narrator temporizes: "Well and good, just be patient," and goes on writing.

Except for sensuality, the erotic, and animus toward intellectuals, the themes of the prose microscripts resemble those in the published work of the period. What is different is their distillation into discrete, juxtaposed narrative segments, as well as the greater reliance on aural and imagistic association and variation to enrich the subtext. Part of the considerable challenge the microscripts pose for the reader lies in identifying their point of view. The extensive reference in the texts, the basis of which is Walser's complex and pervasive irony, makes determination of point of view difficult and sometimes inappropriate. Admittedly, the tension in the narrator-author between self-assertion and revocation of self in the instances cited is alleviated by the transparent irony, although here, too, the passages are not as unidimensional as their isolation from the text might suggest. Walser's irony issues from the narrator-author, who is both its principal exponent and its principal object in works where emphasis on language and theme regularly subvert plot as subject matter. It is the peculiarity and the function of this irony to enlarge and revitalize its object by loosening it from the confines of convention through shifts of perspective. Like the ambulatory, self-styled workaday poet more frequently found in the published work, Walser's ironist represents the breadth of actuality inherent in relationships, between human beings, to oneself, to objects, and to intellectual constructs, fractionalized in narration and degree of proximity through spontaneity. Underlying this narrative ebb and flow is the constant in Walser's understanding of reality: the multifarious levels of meaning, motivation, and potentiality in human experience.

The microscripts demonstrate this multifariousness more extensively—and more acutely—than does the published work in combinative narrative forms. Combination embodies the essence of Walser's poetics and the representational intent of his writing. The range of elements brought together, however, makes the microscripts an extended exercise in oppositional reading—that is, a reading that separates aesthetic and intellectual response from a categorical critical evaluation of the verbal agility, the humor, the story line, the narrative interruptions, the self-assessments and commentary the narrator mobilizes.

The greater freedom from constraints in the microscripts utilizes the device of a narrator and an addressee to achieve Walser's narrative strategm to deconstruct the premises of literature by withholding from the addressee-reader the security of a unitary interpretation of the text. The texts' variously engendered immediacy—nearly every opening of a microscript text arouses reader response—engages the reader with a narrator who proves unreliable. Walser thus provides the basis for access to his work while asking the reader to identify with the figurative representations of reality as shaped by the narrator's own variable proximity to the elements of the work.

Walser makes his narrators culpable, whether as literary provocateurs, as confessants, or as ironists in masked self-projections who invalidate the linguistically inspired bond to the reader. Fergo, for example, is taken with the notion of writing an essay on the Middle Ages emphasizing the Children's Crusades. Here Walser is alluding to his own age and to the recurrent motif of imputed childishness, as well as making an authorial cross-reference to microscripts such as the one beginning "Important people call me a child and I would be ill-mannered if I too didn't believe it" (498/i).

The mock-earnest fear of a day of literary and personal reckoning is strikingly exploited in a text beginning "Soon the limit will be breached. The way I carry on and have carried on, no one else has and no one else shall" (265/i). Confessional and self-negating in stance, the text eddies around an unpaid sum of money for board, which an artist will airily disregard. Intertwined in the confessant-author's narrative is his beloved, presently estranged because of his inconsiderateness and selfishness. She treats him now "with cold respect." Nevertheless, he looks behind the window curtain before going to bed, to see if she is hiding there. At night, at his reading and writing desk, "this high fire of longing" for her ignites. Awakening after a good night's sleep, however, the artist, "the friend of the rhythmical," awakens too, "and the poor, shy person hides himself from the dance-gifted one." The verbal web of the text is drawn tight in a coda driven by the rhetoric of self-interrogation, the conclusion of which reads: "Why can't I ever find myself unbearable? How come I put up with the kind of gentleman I am? I would never have thought of this business with the money for board. It only occurred to him, this him in the middle of me, this inspiration catcher, whom I never, never give refuge. I assure you that personally, for my part, I would almost never laugh. It is he who is always full of laughter, the fairytaler."

Both the suspect character of writing and the commitment to writing are deep rooted in Walser and run at crosscurrents through the prose microscripts. The text above is an example of how the stratagems for separating writing from the person of the writer become more diversified even as questions about the nature and the legitimacy of art become more insistent.

A topically related text, one of the longest in the microscripts and one of the unqualified abreactions in them, is a pained denunciation of society's cultivated, accepted writers in the form of a fictive letter to a female reader of his works who wants to spare her fiancé every care so that he can concentrate on writing. The correspondent does not address the alleviation of cares, but rather undertakes a frontal attack on his contemporaries' understanding of literature and their culture, accusing "all these exceptionally well-read people" of "lacking entirely a fortuitous relationship to everyday life." Because their reading and writing is focused on the past, he rejects their understanding of Verlaine, rejects the comparison made of his own work with that of Dostoyevsky, and disallows their lament that our age cannot produce a Casanova since they are incapable of accommodating what is common and vulgar. Lacking the strength of soul to respect their immediate surroundings, "they continually conduct a secret war against whatever is alive." "I'm talking about people . . ," the letter continues, "who can't believe that a Marcel Proust could exist anywhere but in Paris, about people who believe in the famous, but not in themselves" (195).

The distinction between the correspondent and the cultivated is historically justified but is undercut by the relentlessness of Walser's self-examination when, in other texts, the narrator concedes he himself is one of the cultivated when he is thinking, or that the preoccupation with literature has "aestheticized" him.

An analogous, still more critical question is posed by language, or music—the recurrent metaphor through all of Walser's work for the combinative power and resonant beauty of language. Customarily, the reliance on language is complete. One example follows a bravura opening in a text that goes on to concede that "although I can hardly say what I mean by that, you'll agree, won't you, that it sounds so beautiful and my words can perhaps be compared with female dancers who—perhaps somewhat grotesquely—succeed in conveying the trashing and ragging of everything ideal" (132/i). An ironically negative reflection of a comparable estimate of language occurs in a story of deferred affection, where the rejected lover's faults include unabating astonishment at the capabilities of language. Yet, as was seen in the distancing of self from "the dance-gifted one . . . this him in the middle of me," Walser subjects language itself, the ground of his artistry, to the dialectic of ironic honesty. The microscripts, for the first time, show this ground significantly threatened.

An antithetical stance that also conveys some of Walser's native tempestuousness is found in a fragmentary letter by Ursula the Wild One. Ursula addresses a gentleman who had once asked her for a letter (read: prose piece) that would entertain without being offensive. She writes in an elevated, ardent style, citing her regard for the "cultivation . . . which our moral development imposes on us" (272/ii). But "the undersigned disempowered," as she refers to herself, wants to point to concessions already made: "Now, I'm first of all going to tell you that I've forbidden myself every fuller joy, every unguarded, every unreflected surrender to the being that permeates me." The letter breaks off where Ursula claims her correspondent disregards the weight of personal destiny in those "who want to preserve what is valuable from what is evil and what is good from what is evil."

Walser's characterization of his prose as "the shorter or longer chapters of a realistic novel . . . a first-person book" is in the microscripts more manifestly the literary struggle for acceptance as citizen and artist waged from the vantage point of irony. Characteristically for Walser, its framework, not its particulars, is tact and concomitant circumspection. The elegant, accommodating, and understated formulations for instinct and strong emotion, the stylization of insights as pathos effect intellectual and emotional reverberations in the reader. Where Walser's elegance is perceived to overlap with the elegance of the cultivated, "fictions" threaten writing; hence the implicit and explicit questions on the veracity of art.

Representative of the benign form of the extent to which writing is lying is one narrator's observation that lying is "certainly our nicest trait," it makes us affective, while frankness is repulsive "because we are so cultivated, so cultured" (256). More foreboding is the premature happy ending in a tale about a child with a painful illness whose Jack-Sprat-and-fat-wife parents serve her "religion and sauerkraut," that is, put her in the care of a sectarian whose doctrine of robust health the daughter dutifully repeats when her parents ask how she feels, until she dies and is to receive her rewards in heaven. In the coda, the story is turned around when the narrator—on another microscript sheet —says: "But there I go politely lying again." He reports that the girl is in fact still alive, still poor and sick, still confessing weekly to the "commander of her conscience," "still not a very nice girl" for giving her parents so little joy. The narrator's gloss concludes the story: "This is a case I'm proud of. Naturally [the girl] was telling the truth and naturally that's what pleases me most about the whole thing" (517/iii; 190/i).

Another text, a defense of honesty and an evocation of Walser's vulnerability as artist and citizen in Switzerland, progresses through a confession of errors and misdemeanors to an elliptical expression of an oppositional ethos. Admitting at the outset his "horror" at the tactlessness that permits so much lying in his writing, the narrator appeals to "human kindness": "don't, please, demand too much of me." He subscribes to the "view that we can't ever advance too far in honesty, which has to be a cultural factor of the first order." Subsequent attestations of honesty in the text include references to Russia: "Didn't I recently shout 'Gotthelf is taking all the tricks. Russia and Gotthelf!'[6] at a gathering of honestly striving souls?" While the narrator maintains that "for reasons of health" he can't go into all sorts of complaints "which people direct at me," he does confess "with bliss" that he is ashamed of himself for the words "A toast to Russia, Cheers!" shouted one evening in the city's crowded, "charming arcades." "Do I know Moscow?" the narrator asks. "No. Do I know Crimea? No. But I do know a painter from whom a lady ordered a drawing which she returned to him saying it didn't sing to her heart" (249/ii).

The range of discourse in the prose microscripts and their transfigured portrayals of self make them invaluable for a balanced assessment of Walser. They substantiate the conciliatory dimension in his work as a singular contribution to experimental prose of the twenties. The great number of self-described love stories in the microscripts, often based on material "read up on" or "appropriated," are illustrative. Together they constitute a Walserian semantics of desire, one sublimated into literature as paradigms of moral irony. Shaped as comedy, they particularize, analyse, comment on, or parody the flux of love: love failed, indifferent, self-destructed, or conventionally triumphant. They limn the obstacles we make for love, whether as reflections of our pretensions and ambitions, as conformist victims of what the figure of Don Juan calls "society's eternally whispering prudery" (476/ii), of our delusions, or fear of engagement.

All the faithful Emil can do when his Nathalie reveals that his innocence has driven her to faithlessness is to threaten her with the army-issue weapon he keeps at home. A well-to-do girl brought up in a "vanity case" (524/i) promptly falls in love and marries a handsome Italian after arriving in Rome to join an organization combating the exploitation and seduction of women. She turns frigid when he does not mend his ways, although the narrator ventures to say that he is not a bad sort. Even if some of the stories are based on the penny novels and romances Walser says he read regularly in Bern, his adaptations undercut the conventions of love. The typified figures are made still more emblematic by names like Eulalia, Herz, Schmiss, or Figurina; names are changed from one episode to the next, or figures from sequentially narrated stories in the same text reappear in stories not originally their own. An amorous straw widow—upon seeing her husband, following his return from the Urals, eat with a knife—is moved to resume—and to flaunt—her affair with the factory owner Herr Berger. The cluster of glossing names given her include Frau Frühlingsfeld, (Mrs. Springfield), Frau Herrenfeld (Mrs. Gentlemenfield), Frau Saatfeld (Mrs. Seedfield), and the given name Zulima, a pun on Swiss dialect "glue shut."

Without disparaging the reality of love or discounting the potency of happiness, Walser skews the language of decorum he controls so beautifully to uncover emotion outside the province of decorum and emotion at odds with the conventions of noble sentiment.

Unconventional emotions in explicitly erotic texts were probably not intended for publication, although the narrator in "The Green Spider," a collage of two femmes fatales, states that he is on orders to make fun of eroticism despite the proven fact "that I too tremble at it" (260/iii). An avowedly provocative text—"I mean it to elicit indignation" (264/iii)—deals with the attraction the mistress of an estate feels for the wife of a portrait painter she engages. The lady persuades the painter's wife they should show one another their *dessous*. When they do so, they embrace with shrieks of delight while "the painter forbearingly accommodated himself" (264/iii) when informed his wife would now be spending a lot of time with the lady. In other texts, latent eroticism defines the unspoken relation of the author to women and to lack of initiative as a writer. The "tragic love" of Lizzi Duttweiler, a farmer's daughter in Missuri [*sic*], coincides with the Walser persona as a black. Lizzi is carrying the child of Ralf, a Negro slave from Florida, who, as "rumor has it" (187/iii; 190/ii), peeled potatoes in Indiana and has now run away from the Duttweiler farm as well. With preternatural sensibility Lizzi believes she hears in the rocking and shaking of her unborn child the voice of an "upstart." Rarely is the narrator as unguarded as in this aside between two erotic tales: "Might our sexuality be a homeland for man and might many of us feel ourselves expelled from it?" (515/ii; 516).

The question is answered provisionally in another text that bespeaks the wisdom of renunciation and the primacy of an artistic calling. In a letter to a female friend of his beloved, a friend who he suspects may never be loved and is thus free of love's strictures, the narrator contemplates forswearing love to replace it with respect for everyone.

Walser's literary adaptation of libido to comedy is urbane by remove. The deeper experience of sensuality resides for him in art and the artist's existence as verbal dancer, for whom art is "mother and father and brother and friend and mistress unto himself" (265), the self-professed believer in beauty and cruelty. Specifics in individual texts and a group of them in their entirety are sensualistically, almost ritualistically bloody. In "The Barbarian Woman" the narrator is the privileged emissary and votary of a cruel subjugator of a people "unwise enough" to have ignored her domain (255/ii). This fantasy and others like it aim to confirm the province of art and to unclog and replenish its sources. Doubts notwithstanding, Walser's narrator resists the diminution of art: "Is it really the task of art to become weaker by reason of those who are weaker? Holy Sebastian!" (480a/i).

However varied the personae that adumbrate renewal at the sources, as one privy to the Empress of the World, as Ursula the Wild One, as renouncing Nubian lover, as musing admirer of "the coarse yet gracious eroticism of Negro melodies" (515/ii), or as an Ali Baba ravished and in thrall to his passion for "the cruelest of all mistresses" (524/ii), Walser will not compact with the denigration of man. In a haunting text dealing with "primeval things" (480b/iv), the narrator rejects Countess Circe's offer to free him from his intellectualism by becoming her partner, to write the stories she would tell him.

As a final example of Walser's literary formulation of conciliation, or what he calls "the question of peace," in a vaguely topical text on postwar Europe, I would like to cite the conclusion of a long microscript that dramatizes provisional surcease from ideas lived out as literary personae, a respite that would precede reclaiming the rich preserve Walser so assiduously staked out as artist in his bourgeois homeland. The initially associative text begins with an already cited allusion to the narrator's putative childishness; it only assumes sustained focus when the narrator speaks of money owed his beloved. He had promised himself to present her some seven thousand francs as an outright gift, but the money was already spent. The text moves away from this "embezzlement" to take up the theme of writing, various diurnal events, and the details of an oppressive dream incorporating narrative fragments from earlier in the text. The conclusion envisions satisfaction of the debt—with no mention of money—as an "official act of unification" out in the open country, "close to the fields I had worked with a hoe." His beloved will be accompanied by a party that includes "people from elegant circles." One of the beloved's attendants will hand the narrator "an inventory" of the ways in which he had obligated himself to her. The narrator's attendants would be people who are amused at their insight into the need to be supercilious. "Then, in plain view of all the witnesses, a kind of reconciliation-embrace would come about, which will be of completely ceremonial nature." The narrator would leave only after the appeased beloved had left the meeting place in her carriage.

Walser's expressive self-stagings of the narrator-author's fall as confession, and recovery as comedy, give substance to Martin Walser's view that the irony in Robert Walser is at least the equal of Kafka's in its emancipatory impulse.[7] Walser's self-stylization as marginal actor in life's theater vies with the somnambulistic certitude of the artist as emblems of his receptiveness to and his absorption of the fabric of the society with which he wished to identify himself. In one of his later aphorisms, Kafka writes that confession and lying are identical, for "one can only communicate what one is not, consequently, a lie." All that this self-deprecatory truth seeker will allow is that "a certain inexpressible truth" exists "in the chorus" of lies.[8] The microscript prose texts suggest that, for Walser, truth lies in the contradictory confessions of self-revelation presented as fictions.

Christopher Middleton

# A Parenthesis to the Discussion of Robert Walser's Schizophrenia

It occurs to me that we might risk taking a categorical leap away from the notion of schizophrenia. The term blankets a malaise that is in any case a clinical enigma—and the blanket is somewhat moth eaten, too. I suggest that Walser presents us with the spectacle, purely and simply, or in aspects variously displaced, of a liminoid personality in action.

To be more precise: he represents to us strikingly liminoid traits in bursts of idiosyncratic prose. By *liminoid* I mean that a particular vein of imaginative energy, with which certain artists are endowed, tends to undulate or oscillate back and forth across regions of the mind, provinces of expression that are normally marked by heavy distinctions, barriers, borders, boundaries, and thresholds (*limes* being Latin for threshold). The supposedly less nervous, less peculiarly imaginative person tends to stand foursquare enough on one side or another of any threshold. Of Walser's madness, one might say that it became apparent only after he had slipped, or graduated, from the liminoid to the lunatic. Or else one might say that he was progressively victimized into lunacy ("suicided by society," perhaps, in Artaud's ugly phrase). Either way, the "humble servant" outdid himself.

Walser's prose, then, might be viewed as a subtle record of the mastery—and the lapses—with which a great artist of the word patrols the hairline fractures, the delicate intervals, also the dizzying gulfs, between segments into which human beings categorically carve the world of their experience—individual and social. Does this not happen more often than we might think? Rilke's poetry matures the moment he lights on intervals, interstices, fugitive threshold situations, as the proper leverage for imaginative work, as volatile nowheres in which reality is to be most singularly sensed. That is the reality that Wallace Stevens conceived of as not external or solid or even immediate, but "a shade that traverses / A dust, a force that traverses a shade."

Or consider the improbable fusion in the singing voice of Kiri Te Kanawa, of freedom and power, grace and force, ecstasy and control. In Walser's case, one might think of the acrobat and his wobble, or of the bicyclist's inconspicuous, near-miraculous recoveries of balance by means of which he propels his vehicle. Walser was able to sustain his own exhilarating kinetic wobble through self-doubt, despair, nightmare, and spates of stubborn work, not to mention poverty and rejection, until about 1929. Then the wobble began to catch up with him and to shake him. Could that be because, given such a liminoid imagination, nothing in life is ever quite resolved?

So, on one hand we might have before us a paradigmatic liminoid personality. At large in that paradigm, on the other hand, there seems also to be what Jungians (notably Marie von Franz) have called a *puer aeternus*: an individual or innocent imagination, who has so much "eternity" lodged in his nature that he hardly ever does what ordinary folks resolve to do—grow up. The *puer aeternus*, for all his radiance and vitality, for all his courage and tormenting self-insistence, often gets into trouble at about the age of fifty. (The "midlife crisis" is less troubling for him because he knows he is not getting old.) Briefly, before we opt for any standard clinical description of Walser in 1929, we might recognize this liminoid elfin Walser who stubbornly declines to grow up, to accommodate himself to society, who refuses to be *tamed*.

In addition, I suggest that the *puer aeternus* Walser might be contrasted with another one: Goethe. Once in a blue moon a *puer aeternus* remains intact and reaches an advanced age with his creative powers not much diminished. Goethe did so. The grand maturity of his mind, tested and seasoned by a multitude of external interests and profound experiences, including responsiveness to the radiance of the erotic (which does not seem to have figured in the script of Walser's fortune), trained and transformed, and was not impeded by, his unquenchable gusto, his ability to be almost constantly emergent, variously to refresh himself.

Even then, we should not forget how problematic Goethe was, as a *puer aeternus* of the passions: how scatty he could be, how angry he could get, how biased, how despairing, how unkind. The contrast I am suggesting becomes clearer if one pictures a reading at which the young Weimarian Goethe and the Berliner Walser are billed to perform, before a mixed German and Swiss public. Goethe carries it off with splendor, improvising, parodying, serious, mysterious, entertaining, and generally confident, clad in his green huntsman's mantle and with his dark Italianate eyes aglow. But Walser? His voice does not carry, he cannot externalize the supple vocality intrinsic to his text, he cannot mask his unliterary accent, and his enunciation is as drab as his threadbare clothes.

This resistance, the defiance that consorts with the liminoid personality, prohibits or inhibits even simulation of concern for proprieties. Sometimes, too, the defiance mushrooms into self-love or "inflated consciousness," which even when craving for alterity renders all other subjectivities opaque and schematic. (Here a nihilism lends a hand.) But when a crisis does come, or when that which was always in a condition of crisis is no longer sustained by fabulous gyrations and fascinating volatility, then breakdown can occur. No longer can one oscillate and undulate fruitfully from one side of a threshold to another. Even so, was not Walser still writing at his best in 1932? The Cézanne essay is not just ironically charming, it is glowing, balanced, incisive. Perhaps Walser was only mad in flashes, only mad to the extent that he resolved to accept, with a shrug of the shoulders, wryly, as is the way with a *puer aeternus*, the designation "mad" that flowed as naturally from doctors and decorum as his own prose had flowed from him. (Yet there can be no doubt: he was crushed by suffering.)

To that extent he had been flirting with madness for a long time. Consider certain strange sentences in the earlier Walser (around 1910), sentences of a kind that Kafka probably noticed—later modulating and intensifying what Walser had hit on, and inflecting that kind of structure with what he took from Kleist. I mean the kind of sentence that begins with an assertion, then qualifies it, then modifies the qualification, then soon is unraveling itself through (typically) interstitial details, and eventually it cancels itself out in a labyrinth of negative/positive qualifications. (The cancellation may resemble the portrayal of hidden and hollow spaces in Cubism.) This appears, at all events, to be the general structure of Kafka's "sliding paradox"—first identified as such by Gerhart Neumann. The initial positive modulates into a negative, to expose, bit by bit, the shimmer of uncertainty that overlays the threshold of so much verbal representation. The sentence so structured vibrates with volatile personality, and it has a distinct voice. It carries signatures of incalculable interior shiftings and foldings, graspings and lettings-go of the volatile liminoid imagination—its makeshifts, its dubiety, its permanent condition of emergence—Piaget's "standing wave" structure. Liminoid personalities, I suspect, have an exceptionally and sometimes painfully keen sense of these things, of the variable differentials that contrive language, contrive the undulant psychodrome in which language does its act or clowns around. There is another problem here. You might say that Thomas Mann, too, is liminoid, with his antitheses and tensions, and his antagonisms—thematic or formal contrast effects. Yet with Mann there is an immensely intricate intellectual superstructure to the narrative; a massive culture is enshrined there. Perhaps that mass serves to cushion the authorial imagination. With Walser it is obviously otherwise. He is footloose and barefoot, and he dances rather than plods. His dance is that of an autodidact (albeit he read widely), exposed, boyish, defenseless, wholly dependent on a spontaneity that eludes, as much as it challenges, the sequential determinacy of ideas. It is amazing that he held out as long as he did against the loneliness, horror, disappointments, and maybe against a cruel death-wish that he fended off with all the zest and crispness of sensibility at his command.

As for the term *liminoid*, I must mention two books by Victor Turner: *The Ritual Process*, about African rites, and *Image and Pilgrimage*, on pilgrimage rites in Mexico, Spain, and Ireland. Victor Turner reserves the word *liminal* for properly religious festive events, like Carnival, where norms and values are overthrown for a measure of time so that individuals and groups alike may be ventilated, purged of grievance, ennui, repressed urges, and so forth. In liminal rites, people traverse thresholds in consciousness, they cross a *limes* and arrive, momentarily, or maybe for a week, through the mediation of sundry colorful or ascetic disciplines, in an alternative reality (as long as all goes well). Under those changed conditions, in the alterity contrived by the rites in which all who are present participate imaginatively, the undersides and othersides of things and selves are glimpsed; a reversed image of reality is brought to blossom in the mind. The liminal may shade into the liminoid: the latter term is reserved by Turner for enterprise in learning and the arts, artisanal concerns, and so forth. In the liminoid category of experience we may reach peaks of imaginative and intellectual clarity at which, creatively enough, we again penetrate the miasmas of normative codes, arrive at an unpremeditated insight, behold the world afresh, even fall in love again with the look and spirit of the world—but all this from beyond delusion (as long as deliverance from it lasts).

Yet the liminoid imagination is dangerous. It is dangerous to others and to the personality that is its vehicle. Rites, as everyone knows, are wonderful mechanisms for releasing dangerous energy and for insulating it. Practice in the arts is rather less wonderful, and besides, the poet stands naked and alone in the lightning storm. He does not only witness the carnival, he creates it, and for it he invents a language that can extend from the commonplace to the monstrous, from the familiar to the unknown.

One certainly burrows into such matters while trying to translate Walser. Repeatedly observed in his short prose, for instance, is an extension of the picaresque tradition (*carnivalization* in Bakhtin's terms) into a province where lyrical subjectivity, mysterious as ever, not narrative mass, is the measure of things. Liminoid and picaresque, this prose has a mobility rare enough in itself, although it distinguishes other German-language writers, who, in whatever mood, are masters of *brio*—Büchner, Heine, Nietzsche. The mystery in Walser cannot be "boiled down" to anything, but it can be sought in his rhythm. His rhythm is unlike that of his avatars. Indeed, he makes the most of that inaudible, nonapparent function of language that we call syntax. Mallarmé regarded syntax as the principle of motion, creative motion, in language. A radiant spirit dances in the body of the vocables. That spirit, did it eventually dance Walser clean off the map of words? Had society suicided him, at last? No. He just decided, let us say, that he had had enough, done enough. It was time to be mad, a duller carnival perhaps, but one that might diminish the agony of a future, of uncertain survival through a future. So then, he might as well try it.

Winfried Kudszus

# Walser's Silence

Walser's writings translate well into English and other languages. He appears in translation in the first place. He is a translator of himself into his works. Nowhere do we read him in the original. His silence after 1933 suggests more of a presence than does his writing. "I'm not here to write, but to be mad,"[1] he says of his postliterary existence. "To write" had become an ever more complicated *process*; "to be mad" implies a sense of *being*. Schizophrenia upside down? Was Walser in the madness of his silence more authentic than in the inaccessibility of his writing? I will focus here on a narrative process and its link with questions of identity and illness. The words and terms at my disposal will emerge and fade. Diagnostic issues will dissolve. Walser should be left alone.

The narrator in his "Essay on Freedom" is not Walser, nor is he sure of his own identity.[2] Moving along borderlines of language and perception, he approaches his room one evening. He tries to take us along. "With the reader's leave, or rather that of the readeress, whom the writer always pictures as a lovely person, well-disposed," the narrator refers to "puzzles," or, more accurately, to "irritabilities," "Irritiertheiten." To some extent he is letting down his guard. His thoughts on freedom have approached the flow of his dreams. He has just proposed a view of freedom beyond rational constraints: "Freedom wants both to be understood and to be almost continuously not understood; it wants to be seen and then again to be as if it were not there; it is at once real and unreal, and on this point much more might well be said." Dreams and freedom are linked in their fluidity, and they challenge the limits of reality. The textual process proceeds to further explore these limits. Reality and unreality are viewed in relation to freedom and the narrator's boundaries:

One evening I start off homeward and on arriving at the house where I live I see two people, a man and a woman, looking out of the window of my room. Both these unknown people have conspicuously large faces and are quite motionless, a sight possibly apt to make a free person unfree on the spot, in every way. For quite a long time he stares at the people staring, so to speak nonchalantly, down at him, he cannot explain to himself their presence, goes upstairs, intending to ask the inexplicable occupants of his room, as politely as possible, to tell him, if they would be so kind, why they are there, and I walk in, find everything quiet, no persons are there. For a time I do not sense my own person either, I am pure independence, which is not in every way quite what it ought to be, and I ask myself if I am free.

There is a change from the *I* to the *he* and back to the *I*; and a parallel change from just the narrator's presence to the appearance of two people and back to the narrator. The narrator is coming home or rather, trying to. Walser emphasizes the symbolism of the attempt. The entire passage alludes to basic ingredients of human existence, even more visibly in his German "die . . . unbekannten *Menschen*" ("these unknown people"; italics mine) and in the repeated use of "Gestalt" (translated "person"). The narrator who lives alone sees "two people . . . looking out of the window" of his room. In his absence the room, it seems, has opened up in several ways. It has acquired more of an outer dimension. The narrator is looking in on his space turned outside. His dwelling has become a kind of screen or mirror which, in a sense, provides him a view of himself: "these unknown people have conspicuously large faces and are quite motionless." The narrator is absorbed by the picture for "quite a long time." He is "staring." He freezes at the sight of the "unknown" he knows so well. His sense of self is at stake, or rather, it is at the point of potential transformation towards the kind of freedom that emerged with the dreams of the previous passage. The stare, back and forth between him and them, blocks a gaze of recognition. A further movement toward self-discovery *is* a possibility here, congruent with the overall development of the text. "He," who lives alone, however, holds on to the stare which imprisons him further. Walser's "Essay" has arrived at the threshold of personal evolution and "freedom" of perception. Yet "he" does not dare to cross the line, and there is a sense of parental menace, deep-seated and unpronounced, in the two large-faced figures staring down at him in unison. The challenge of recognizing the apparition as a potential opening and a stimulus for self-evolution is buried by the machinery of reflection: "he cannot *explain* to himself their presence, goes upstairs, *intending* to ask the *inexplicable* occupants of his room, as politely as possible, to tell him, if they would be so kind, *why* they are there" (italics mine). As to be expected, no meeting takes place. The narrator has responded to the shock at his window sill by switching to a less personal and more reflective *he*. It is not surprising that his sense of "Gestalt" is gone at the end, "no persons are there. . . . I do not sense my own person either." Yet there is also an element of reflecting on the pitfalls of reflection. The narrator has lost himself and realizes: "I am pure independence, which is not in every way quite what it ought to be, and I ask myself if I am free." Asking this question might suggest a freedom from the kind of reflection that quells the sense of "Gestalt." Such a sense would be linked with an abdication of the concept of "pure independence." The narrator has been transformed into the "pure image of freedom" which, from the very beginning of the essay, was undercut. To some extent the question of whether "I am free" is rhetorical. The text knows better, yet it is energized by the painful stoppage of an evolution towards a more genuine understanding of freedom. Neither at peace with reflection nor at home with personal experience, the narrator is driven at a fast pace through an array of frozen possibilities. He seems part of the process of the work itself, part of the flow of language perhaps. Yet such formulations approximate him only. Or perhaps they catch him, the narrator, while reflecting to some extent the author implied by the work. The narrator, after all, is forced by his role to engage in a considerable degree of revelation, whereas the implied author may reside unseen in the spaces above or between the words and lines. And while the narrator may shrink from the possible evolution of shock into insight, the implied author may be aware. Or, there may be a constellation in between these two, such as would occur if the author of this text were in search of his freedom, experimenting with his narrator and the emerging dialectics of liberation and self-burial. What, finally, if anything, can be said about the man who wrote this piece—the author as different from the implied image created and hidden in the text? But first, let me simply follow the narrator's path to its quick end.

He now presents "a beautiful woman I know," whom we also know, having encountered her or her sister figure earlier in the essay, where she emanated from a "pure image of freedom" as an equally inaccessible "Schätzenswerte, die ich mich beinahe scheue, überhaupt zu erwähnen": "lady to be esteemed, which I almost refrain from mentioning at all." At first sight, not much has changed since then. The beautiful woman is as admirable and "sensitive" as ever, and just as inapproachable. However, a change has occurred in the narrator. Initially he resisted the inaccessibility of "freedom" and sought his strength beneath his apparent frailty: "I am a person who tends to appear to himself more frail than he perhaps actually is." Now, following the shock, and the freezing of the movement towards his own experience, he assumes a comparatively resigned posture. The "free woman" appears from a distance that cannot be bridged, nor does she now spark movement. The narrator's tone is relatively serious, and to the detriment of irony as it were, even somewhat philosophical: her "Freiheit . . . [ist] ein Wesen . . . , das dadurch gestört wird, dass man ihre Beschaffenheit nicht in Betracht zieht"; her freedom is "something that is troubled by any failure to consider how it is constituted."

The final paragraph, a single sentence, has a different tone. It delights in "all the unfreedoms internal to freedom." The inaccessible concept is now enjoyed "by none but a connoisseur and gourmet of freedom." A related lightness pervades the final definition: "freedom is difficult"; in German: "die Freiheit an sich schwierig ist," "freedom *as such*," a weighty, philosophical formulation, yet lightened by syntactical ambivalence. "As such," "an sich" may also belong to "difficult," "schwierig," and thus deflate the significance of those complexities. "Freedom," it is further stated with a trace of mock philosophy, "is difficult *and produces difficulties*," "und *daher* Schwierigkeiten macht" (italics mine). Having shifted the emphasis from the concept to its more tangible manifestations, the narrator is free to *taste* freedom or rather the bits and pieces of unfreedom wrapped in it. He even manages a philosophical spicing à la Novalis, recalling the romantic *Monolog* on creativity free from authorial intent: "perhaps there sprang from my mouth an insight."

Yet is this gourmet still the narrator we knew, who labored with conceptual barriers and froze at the shock of his potential change? Certainly, he did not change *in* the text, but perhaps the essay as a whole is a mask allowing the narrator to feast on his readers? Or is it the perspective of a different person, say, of the implied author, which emerges at the end? Of course, it is the narrator who keeps deliberating; but what if, at the end, he turns into the implied author's marionette, speaking of things he did not comprehend during the play? I will not try to resolve these questions, for, as Christopher Middleton has suggested, drawing on T. S. Eliot, Walser's "network" is "too finely spun . . . to 'allow entrance to an idea.'"[3]

Nor does Robert Walser enter into the text in a definable way. The wisdom of the implied author, or of the narrator at the end, may well be his; but probably not. The text, twisted, multileveled, and even inconsistent as it is, does not reveal a final point of reference. Even its last paragraph, right at the beginning, plants a seed of disbelief: "I hope I may be believed if I permit myself to say . . ." Walser: a nonappearance in the broken evolution of his text and in the hardly reconcilable voices emanating from its various paragraphs. Just as ideas do not measure up to his texts, he himself refuses to be grasped.

Walser, the person; his invention, the implied author of the text; then, the narrator, twice removed, so to speak, from the author himself; and then, the splitting and self-alienation that the narrator experiences. My attempt to discuss these textual and more than textual figures and their locations has left me with a dynamics of the essay yet also with a void. Prose at the edge of silence not only takes critical categories to their limits, it blurs boundaries much needed for a stable view of reality. Everything and everyone seems in flux in Walser's world. Flux and absence characterize his writing to the end in 1933, when, as an author, he fell silent for the remaining decades of his life.

Schizophrenia?[4] We know of Walser's hallucinations and of his bouts with extreme anxiety. We see in his style and his images various elements of instability, including the multiplicity of meanings in the text at hand. Yet, throughout his writing, Walser stays on top, speaks from increasingly invisible locations beyond the textual dilemma. We hear, perhaps, his laughter, or its opposite; we experience, and occasionally miss his ironies; beyond the level of narration he eludes our grasp. And yet we grope for answers. If Walser was overcome at times by his voices and his fears, schizophrenic episodes perhaps, he nevertheless remained himself, the author, the silent one, the voice beyond hallucination. To the end of his writings and in his silence we sense *him, his* tone, *his* ability to rise, in pain and in mockery, above even his fears, or to descend into them. There are stories and photographs of Walser's later years, and there are his own stories and images. Looking at all of these traces, we need not freeze in diagnostic terror. Let me draw a picture of his later writing, specifically of his "Essay on Freedom."

I see a landscape of uncertain and swiftly shifting boundaries. No firm lines of demarcation are visible. The borders between dream and reality, one figure and another, one concept and another are blurred. It is a frightening and at the same time promising scenery. "Freedom," the main concern here, "wants to be seen and then again to be as if it were not there," and this double demand propels the narrator's thoughts into various directions with great rapidity. So quickly does his mind move that at times the images approach a strobe light effect, a rhythmically fragmented quality. The mind at work here moves faster than feeling. There *is* feeling in the text, yet it is spotty and does not develop into an emotionally differentiated texture. If anything, emotions are *anticipated*, and so are various reactions, including those of the reader or the "readeress." Quick movement and anticipation create, in this Walser piece and in others, a kind of ideogram. Energized by an underlying turbulence—fear, alienation, shifting lines of demarcation—writing here moves at the borders of imagination and intellectual cohesion. Its trajectory leads through the no-man's-land between reality and dreams, sanity and madness, consciousness and forgetting. The hand tracing its rapid course swiftly oscillates, in the micrographic manner, unreadable at first, of Walser's later years. Micrographic writing: an instrument of borderline exploration. In borderline territory, forces of disintegration and reconstruction clash and interact and recombine. Often, and certainly in Walser's writing, it is a question of life and death, both springing from the shadowy meeting grounds of existence and formlessness. It is also a question of writing. Robert Walser, in his writing, knew and sensed the death implied in the fixed configurations of words and images. He also probed the void engendered by the absence of such configurations. Death here and there; but also life, the swift journey into language and out of it, simultaneously. Walser's prose probes uncertain spaces restlessly, not coming to a halt, moving along and beyond and back again across borderlines which, in the process, shift and change along with their explorer.

To some extent, then, I have described what current psychiatry terms borderline symptoms. Yet let me refuse entrance to this idea, too. In Walser's prose the sense of control and artistry, combined with self-mockery and twists of absurdity, creates a distance between rapid shifts of exploration and hidden zones of reference. The narrator's explorations oscillate back and forth across boundaries of individuality and controlled perception, but his journey, as I have shown, is not his own. The shadowy realms he probes are seen from yet another perspective. The narrator's borderline movements and the excitement he creates are observed from more secure and more isolated authorial quarters. Viewed from these quarters, a kind of spectacle takes place in the text and in its interaction with us, the readers. The further we are drawn into the laughs and frights of the theater of words, the more invisible and autonomous the stage director becomes. He watches the borders, looks at them as into a mirror reflecting himself and nothing but himself. Nothing at all and yet everything. Beyond the narrative configurations visible in the text lies a territory of fear and freedom. Freedom in every sense and countersense of the word explored in the text. The grandiose freedom of an untouchable, yet to be admired figure; the "un-freedoms" of the same figure wanting to be seen and touched and cherished; the freedom of Narcissus who sees himself only and yet desires to be seen; the freedom of the mirror and the mirrored and the shattered mirror. Walser's writing was his mirror. His silence is Walser himself.[5]

# Chronology

1878    Robert Otto Walser is born in Biel, Switzerland, on April 15.

1892    Leaves school at the age of fourteen.

1892–95 Apprenticeship with a bank in Biel, the Bern Kantonalbank.

1894    His mother dies on October 22.

1895    Five months in Basel, subsequently in Stuttgart where his brother Karl, the painter and scene decorator, was living. Futile attempts to become an actor.

1896    Returns to Switzerland. Lives in Zurich for the next ten years. Frequent changes of address and employment.

1897    Travels to Berlin at the end of November.

1898    A selection of his poems appears in the Bern newspaper *Sonntagsblatt des Bund*.

1901    In Munich in September. Visits the writer Max Dauthendey in Würzburg.

1902    In Berlin in January, then after a brief stay with his sister Lisa in Täuffelen on Lake Biel, returns to Zurich.

1903    Works for an engineer called Dubler in Wädenswil, on Lake Zurich, an experience he will later draw on in *The Assistant* (*Der Gehülfe*).

1904    His first book, *Fritz Kocher's Essays* (*Fritz Kochers Aufsätze*) is published by Insel Verlag, Leipzig.

1905    Moves to Berlin in March. Lives there with his brother Karl. Position as servant at Dambrau Castle in Upper Silesia from October until the end of the year.

1906    Returns to Berlin at the beginning of January. Writes the novel *The Tanner Siblings* (*Geschwister Tanner*).

1907    Completes *The Assistant* (*Der Gehülfe*) in June or July.

1908    Writes *Jakob von Gunten*.

1909    Little is known of the circumstances of Walser's life from 1909 to late 1912.

1912    Prepares two volumes for publication. *Essays* (*Aufsätze*) and *Stories* (*Geschichten*) published by Kurt Wolff in 1913 and 1914 respectively.

(This compilation of biographical data is indebted to the pioneering work of Jochen Greven and Jörg Schäfer)

| 1913 | Returns to Switzerland in March. After brief stays with his sister Lisa, who worked in an asylum at Bellelay, and with his father in Biel, he moves into an attic room in the Hotel Blaues Kreuz in Biel in which he lives for the next seven years. |
|------|------|
| 1914 | His father dies on February 9. Prepares the collection of prose *Small Compositions (Kleine Dichtungen)* for which he receives a prize from the Women's League to Honor Rhenish Writers. Outbreak of First World War. Periods of military service. |
| 1916 | Completes the story "The Walk" in September. *Prose Pieces (Prosastücke)* appears in Zurich. His brother Ernst dies in the Waldau asylum near Bern on November 17. |
| 1917 | Puts together the collection *Small Prose (Kleine Prosa)* and completes *A Poet's Life (Poetenleben)*. |
| 1918 | Completes manuscript of *Sea Landscape (Seeland)*. |
| 1919 | In March completes work on the novel *Tobold*, of which only a fragment survives. His brother Hermann dies on May 1. |
| 1921 | Moves to Bern in January. For some months assistant librarian of the State Archives in Bern. In November completes work on the novel *Theodor* of which, again, only a fragment survives. |
| 1925 | His last book *The Rose (Die Rose)* published by Rowohlt in Berlin. Works on the novel *The Robber (Der Räuber-Roman)*. The manuscript was long considered lost, but came to light in West Berlin and was first published in 1972. |
| 1929 | Enters the asylum at Waldau near Bern on January 25. |
| 1933 | He is moved to an asylum at Herisau in his native canton of Appenzell-Ausserrhoden. Stops writing. New edition of his novel *The Tanner Siblings*. |
| 1936 | Carl Seelig visits Walser for the first time at Herisau. |
| 1943 | His brother Karl dies. |
| 1944 | His sister Lisa dies on January 7. Seelig becomes his legal guardian and literary executor. |
| 1953 | Seelig begins to publish a series of Walser's *Works in Prose (Dichtungen in Prosa)*. |
| 1956 | Robert Walser dies of a heart attack on Christmas Day while out on a walk in the snow-covered fields. |
| 1966 | The first two volumes of Walser's complete works appear, under the editorship of Jochen Greven (Kossodo Verlag). |
| 1985 | Anticipated publication of two further volumes which have been transcribed from the microscripts at the Robert Walser Archive in Zurich. |

# Notes

## Introduction

1. Walser's *Selected Stories*, trans. Christopher Middleton and others (New York: Farrar, Straus & Giroux, 1982) have since appeared in paperback (New York: Vintage, 1983) along with a reprint (1983) by Vintage Books of *Jakob von Gunten*, trans. Christopher Middleton (Austin: University of Texas Press, 1969).

2. "Meine Bemühungen," in Robert Walser, *Das Gesamtwerk*, ed. Jochen Greven (Zurich/Frankfurt: Suhrkamp Verlag, 1978), 12:431.

3. "Literary Form and Social Hallucination," in Harold Rosenberg, *Discovering the Present: Three Decades in Art, Culture, and Politics*, (Chicago: University of Chicago Press, 1973), 14.

4. See John Barth, "The Literature of Exhaustion," *Atlantic Monthly* 220 (August 1967): 29–34; Gerald Graff, "The Myth of the Postmodernist Breakthrough," *Tri-Quarterly* 26 (Winter 1973): 383–417.

5. J. P. Stern, *Reinterpretations* (New York: Basic Books, 1964), 1.

6. "Eine Art Erzählung," in *Das Gesamtwerk* 12:323.

7. "The Child," trans. Mark Harman, in *Comparative Criticism*, ed. E. S. Shaffer (Cambridge: Cambridge University Press, 1984), 261–64; *Das Gesamtwerk* 3:406.

8. "Ich hatte ein Bedürfnis darnach, zärtlich behandelt zu werden, und es geschah nie." *Das Gesamtwerk* 4:114.

9. "So habe ich mein eigenes Leben gelebt, an der Peripherie der bürgerlichen Existenzen, und war es nicht gut so?" See Carl Seelig, *Wanderungen mit Robert Walser* (Frankfurt: Suhrkamp, 1978), 37.

10. "Würzburg," in *Das Gesamtwerk* 3:43.

11. *Das Gesamtwerk* 3:36. See also "Widman," in ibid., 18.

12. See Robert Mächler, *Das Leben Robert Walsers: Eine dokumentarische Biographie* (Frankfurt: Suhrkamp, 1976), 130–31.

13. "Die Talentprobe," in *Das Gesamtwerk* 1:172.

14. *Das Gesamtwerk* 3:128.

15. Walser, "The Walk," in *Selected Stories*, 69–72; *Das Gesamtwerk* 3:228–32.

16. Robert Walser, *Briefe* (Frankfurt: Suhrkamp, 1979), 18 Jan. 1907, 49.

17. Seelig, *Wanderungen*, 22.

18. *Das Gesamtwerk* 12:431.

19. "Mir fiel nämlich erstens heute früh ein, dass ich eigentlich immer eher sowohl französisch wie russisch als deutsch schrieb." See "Ein dummer Junge," in *Das Gesamtwerk* 11:147.

20. Jean-Jacques Rousseau, *The Reveries of a Solitary*, trans. John G. Fletcher (New York: Burt Franklin, 1971), 112. For a reference in Walser to Rousseau and his retreat on Lake Biel, see "Kombination," in *Das Gesamtwerk* 12:357.

21. "Absichten nach Paris zu reisen durchqueren mich sanft." See *Das Gesamtwerk* 11:97. For a superb evocation of the unruly quartet, Apollinaire, Jarry, Rousseau, and Satie, see Roger Shattuck, *The Banquet Years: The Origins of the Avant-Garde in France* (New York: Vintage, 1968).

22. See Wolf-Dietrich Rasch, *Zur deutschen Literatur seit der Jahrhundertwende* (Stuttgart: Metzler, 1967), 5.

23. Seelig, *Wanderungen*, 101.

24. Walser, *Briefe*, 20 June 1927, 301.

25. Mächler, *Das Leben*, 179–80.

26. *Das Gesamtwerk* 9: 28.

27. Gustav Janouch, *Conversations with Kafka* (New York: Praeger, 1953). For a skeptical scrutiny of Janouch's book, see Eduard Goldstücker, "Kafkas Eckermann?" in *Franz Kafka: Themen und Probleme*, ed. Claude David (Göttingen: Vandenhoeck, 1980), 238–55.

28. Seelig, *Wanderungen*, 97.

29. Mächler, *Das Leben*, 188.

30. Carl Seelig requested the original medical report in 1953 and received a transcript from Morgenthaler, dated 26 January 1929, which records the only examination conducted by Morgenthaler, who writes in the letter to Seelig of 14 July 1954 that he had interviewed Walser "a single time." The document (trans. M. H.) is entitled "Medical Report on Mr. Robert Walser, Author":

"Miss Walser, a teacher in Bellelay came to my office hour on 24 January 1929 and reported that for a good while her brother had been getting more and more depressed and inhibited, was afraid, was hearing voices, and was restless at night. One brother had been a long time in Waldau and died there, another had committed suicide."

"I found Mr. Walser to be markedly depressed and severely inhibited. He had insight into his illness, complained about the impossibility of being able to work, about occasional fear, etc. He responded evasively to questions about being sick of life. He would like to be helped, but would not like to enter an institution, would rather go to his sister in Bellelay. Since on external grounds this was not indicated, and, moreover, since after a short while I became convinced that in his present condition Mr. Walser needs the confines of the institution urgently, as quickly as possible, he is committed to Waldau."

"Fräulein Walser, Lehrerin in Bellelay erschien am 24. Januar 1929 in meiner Sprechstunde und gab an, der Bruder sei seit längerer Zeit immer deprimierter und gehemmter geworden, habe Angst, höre Stimmen und sei nachts unruhig. Ein Bruder sei lange in der Waldau gewesen und dort gestorben, ein anderer habe Selbstmord begangen."

"Ich fand Herrn Walser ausgesprochen deprimiert und schwer gehemmt. Er hatte Krankheitseinsicht, klagte über die Unmöglichkeit arbeiten zu können, über zeitweise Angst usw. Auf Fragen nach Lebensüberdruss antwortete er ausweichend. Er möchte sich wohl helfen lassen, möchte aber nicht in eine Anstalt, sondern zur Schwester nach Bellelay. Da dies aus äussern Gründen nicht angezeigt war, und da ich zudem nach kurzem zu der Überzeugung kam, dass Herr Walser in seinem gegenwärtigen Zustand die geschlossene Anstalt dringend und so rasch als möglich nötig hat, wird er an die Waldau gewiesen." A photographic reproduction of this "report" is included in *Robert Walser: Leben und Werk in Daten und Bildern*, ed. Elio Fröhlich and Peter Hamm (Frankfurt: Insel Verlag, 1980).

31. *Das Gesamtwerk* 4: 235–36.

32. Ibid. 6: 301– 6.

33. Karl Jaspers, *Strindberg and van Gogh: An Attempt at a Pathographic Analysis with Reference to Parallel Cases of Swedenborg and Hölderlin*, trans. Oskar Grunow and David Woloshin (Tucson: University of Arizona Press, 1977), 181.

34. "The Avant-Garde," in Rosenberg, *Discovering the Present*, 75.

35. Sigmund Freud, *Beyond the Pleasure Principle*, ed. James Strachey (New York/London: Norton, 1961), 13–14.

36. Jochen Greven, "Robert Walser—Forschungen," *Euphorion* 64 (March 1970): 112.

37. "Besteht nicht Schriftstellern vielleicht vorwiegend darin, dass der Schreibende beständig um die Hauptsächlichkeit herumgeht." "Der heisse Brei," in *Das Gesamtwerk* 11: 92.

38. *Das Gesamtwerk* 7: 41.

39. Robert Alter, *Partial Magic: The Novel as a Self-Conscious Genre* (Berkeley: University of California Press, 1975). For a discussion of related issues in Walser, see Mark Harman, "Stream of Consciousness and the Boundaries of Self-Conscious Fiction: The Works of Robert Walser," in *Comparative Criticism*, 119–34. For a glimpse of Snowwhite in an era in which alienation has become a self-consciously chic cliché, see Donald Barthelme, *Snowwhite* (New York: Atheneum, 1967).

40. *Das Gesamtwerk* 11: 194. See Irma Kellenberger, *Der Jugendstil und Robert Walser* (Bern: Francke, 1981).

41. Fröhlich and Hamm, *Walser*, 295.

42. Ovid, *Metamorphoses*, 3d. ed., trans. F. J. Miller, Loeb Classical Library, book 3 (Cambridge: Harvard University Press, 1976), 54–55. For a discussion of the case for "narcissistic," in the sense of self-conscious, fiction, see Linda Hutcheon, *Narcissistic Narrative: The Metafictional Paradox* (Waterloo: Wilfred Laurier University Press, 1980).

43. *Das Gesamtwerk* 7: 51.

44. Ibid. 8: 31.

45. Ibid., 17.

46. Ibid. 12: 323.

47. There is good reason to believe that the Walser story "Ovation" included in this selection was the original on which Kafka based the well-known story "Up in the Gallery" in the collection *A Country Doctor*. In Walser's "Ovation" slight stylistic dissonances and ironically repetitive directions to the reader raise doubts about the reality of the idyll. But Walser leaves it up to the reader to determine the effect those nagging reminders have on the performance itself. Since no perspective is made explicit other than that of the reader's imagination, the choice between idyllic and ironic points of view ultimately depends on where the pleasure of the reader lies.

A detailed comparison of the two stories shows that Kafka introduces the perspective of a young visitor to the circus so as to transform Walser's epicurean open form into a dizzying epistemological puzzle. See Karl Pestalozzi, "Nachprüfung einer Vorliebe: Franz Kafkas Beziehung zum Werk Robert Walsers," in *Über Robert Walser*, ed. Katharina Kerr (Frankfurt: Suhrkamp, 1978), 2: 94–114.

48. See Walter Muschg, *Pamphlet und Bekenntnis* (Olten: Walter, 1968), 197–200.

49. Mächler, *Das Leben*, 15–16.

50. *Das Gesamtwerk* 12: 431.

51. William James, *Essays in Radical Empiricism* (Cambridge: Harvard University Press, 1976), 42.

52. Guy Davenport, *Da Vinci's Bicycle* (Baltimore: Johns Hopkins University Press, 1979), 149–85. See also Lisa Ruddick, "Fluid Symbols in American Modernism: William James, Gertrude Stein, George Santayana, and Wallace Stevens," in *Allegory, Myth, and Symbol*, ed. W. Morton Bloomfield (Cambridge, Mass.: Harvard University Press, 1981), 335ff.

53. Martin Jürgens opened new vistas on the late prose in *Robert Walser: Die Krise der Darstellbarkeit* (Kronberg/Taunus: Scriptor, 1973).

54. *Das Gesamtwerk* 3: 374–75.

55. Seelig, *Wanderungen*, 49.

56. *Das Gesamtwerk* 12: 431.

57. Seelig, *Wanderungen*, 44–45.

58. *Das Gesamtwerk* 12: 431–32.

59. James, *Essays*, 42.

**The *Stories* of Robert Walser**

1. Musil is referring to "Der Theaterbrand," a story in which the narrator describes, with what seems like relish, a gruesome conflagration. The utopian counterpoint to the seemingly gratuitous violence in "Theaterbrand" can be seen in the story "A Strange City" in this volume, which also appeared in *Geschichten*, the collection that Musil is reviewing.

**Robert Walser**

1. Alfred Polgar (1873–1955) was considered a master of polished short prose; Franz Hessel (1880–1941) was a novelist and author of impressionistic sketches.

2. Arnold Böcklin (1827–1901) was a Swiss painter; Gottfried Keller (1819–90) was an influential nineteenth-century Swiss novelist.

3. Knut Hamsun (1859–1952) is the pseudonym of Knut Pedersen, the Norwegian novelist.

4. Josef Freiherr von Eichendorff (1788–1857) was a Romantic poet and author of *Aus dem Leben eines Taugenichts* (1826), a lyrical novella describing the wanderings of the child-hero and celebrating the joys of nature. In its time the novella was one of the most widely read works of German Romanticism.

5. Johann Peter Hebel (1760–1826) was a pastor and poet of whom Goethe said that "he makes a peasant of the universe in the most naïve and

charming way." Hebel collected a group of his unassertively didactic stories in *Schatzkästlein des rheinischen Hausfreundes* (1811).

## Unrelenting Style

1. *Je t'adore*, in Robert Walser, *Das Gesamtwerk* (Frankfurt, 1978), 10: 430f.
2. Ibid. 11: 212.
3. Ibid.
4. Ibid. 12: 278.
5. "Robert Walser," in *Über Robert Walser*, ibid., 126ff.
6. Ibid. 11: 212.
7. Ibid. 10: 538.
8. Ibid.
9. Ibid. 2: 346.
10. Ibid. 1: 19.
11. Ibid., 36.
12. Ibid., 100.
13. Ibid., 106.
14. Jean Paul, *Werke* (Munich, 1963), 5: 471.
15. *Das Gesamtwerk* 12: 323.
16. Ibid. 11: 359.
17. Ibid. 9: 64f.
18. Ibid. 1: 319ff.
19. Ibid. 2: 165ff.
20. Ibid. 11: 215.
21. Ibid. 9: 22ff.
22. Ibid., 358.
23. Ibid. 6: 304.
24. Ibid. 10: 188.
25. Ibid., 9.
26. Ibid. 3: 204.
27. Ibid., 403.
28. Ibid., 335.
29. Ibid., 12: 283.
30. Ibid. 10: 132.
31. Ibid. 2: 346.
32. Ibid. 9: 92.
33. Ibid. 8: 282.
34. Ibid., 158.
35. Ibid. 6: 103ff.
36. Ibid. 10: 534.
37. Ibid., 202.
38. Ibid. 11: 185f.
39. Ibid., 262.
40. Ibid.
41. Ibid.
42. Ibid. 1: 294.
43. Ibid. 9: 298.
44. Ibid. 12: 74.
45. Ibid. 8: 318.
46. Ibid. 10: 124.
47. Ibid. 3: 406.
48. Ibid. 10: 202.
49. Ibid., 524.
50. Ibid. 11: 225.
51. Ibid. 10: 409.
52. Ibid., 382f.
53. Ibid., 489.
54. Ibid. 12: 110.
55. Ibid. 2: 315.
56. Ibid., 316.
57. Ibid.

## "Am awake and lie yet in deep sleep"

1. E. Y. Meyer, "Ein grosser Spaziergänger," in *Die Hälfte der Erfahrung* (Frankfurt: Suhrkamp, 1980), 95–99.
2. Max Frisch, *Sketchbook, 1966–1971*, trans. Geoffrey Skelton (New York: Harcourt, Brace, Jovanovich, 1974), 127.
3. Robert Walser, *Jakob von Gunten*, trans. Christopher Middleton (New York: Vintage, 1983), 60. All future quotes from *Jakob von Gunten* will be followed by page references based on this edition.
4. Robert Walser, "Eine Ohrfeige und Sonstiges," in *Das Gesamtwerk* (Zurich: Suhrkamp, 1978), 3: 383. Quotation from the Mark Harman translation in this volume.

5. Max Frisch, "Spuren meiner Nicht-Lektüre," in *Materialien zu Max Frisch "Stiller"*, ed. Walter Schmitz (Frankfurt: Suhrkamp, 1978), 342; and idem, "Die Schweiz als Heimat? *Rede zur Verleihung des Grossen Schillerpreises,"* in *Gesammelte Werke in zeitlicher Folge* (Frankfurt: Suhrkamp, 1976), 6: 512.

6. In "Introduction," by Jochen Schulte-Sasse, in Peter Bürger, *Theory of the Avant-Garde*, trans. Michael Shaw (Minneapolis: University of Minnesota Press, 1984), xii.

7. From Microscript 250, poem in right column, 1: Zurich, Robert Walser Archive.

8. Jochen Greven, "Nachworte: *Jakob von Gunten,"* in *Das Gesamtwerk* 6: 351.

9. Robert Walser, *Der Räuber*, in *Das Gesamtwerk* 6: 181ff. Translation by the author.

10. In 1939 the Kunstgesellschaft Zürich bought this painting from Mme. A. Villard, a private collector in Paris; it is now part of the Kunsthaus collection, Zurich. *Walk in the Forest* was probably painted in 1886 and is thought to be a portrait of Rousseau's wife Clémence who had died a few years earlier. The painting was shown to the public only once before it came to Zurich: at Galerie Bernheim Jeune in Paris in 1912. According to Romy Storrer, registrar at the Kunsthaus Zurich, to whom I am indebted for this information, Robert Walser could have only seen a reproduction of *Walk in the Forest*.

11. Theodore Ziolkowski, "Figuren auf Pump: Zur Fiktionalität des sprachlichen Kunstwerks," in *Akten des VI. Internationalen Germanisten-Kongresses Basel 1980*, ed. Heinz Rupp and Hans-Gert Roloff (Bern: Peter Lang, 1981), 1: 171, 176.

12. William Rubin, *Dada and Surrealist Art* (New York: Harry N. Abrams, 1968), 128. In his introduction to *Jakob von Gunten*, Christopher Middleton observes that Jakob's wooden dialogues remind him of the dialogue in Henri Rousseau's play *La vengeance d'une orpheline russe* (p. 19).

13. André Breton, *Manifestes du surréalisme* (Paris: Gallimard, 1968), 23f., the translation is by W. Rubin, *Dada*, 121.

14. From an undated conversation with his colleague Lothar Schreyer during their Bauhaus years; in Lothar Schreyer, *Erinnerungen an Sturm und Bauhaus* (Munich: Albert Langen, 1956), 171. Similarly in Paul Klee, *Tagebücher* (Cologne: DuMont Schauberg, 1957), no. 905, 1912, p. 276.

15. Robert Walser, "The Walk," in *Selected Stories*, trans. Christopher Middleton et al. (New York: Vintage, 1983), 76. The nightmarish situation can be understood as an attempt on Walser's part to articulate a personal and otherwise repressed fear of being suffocated by the motherly care of his friend whom he addressed in one of his letters as "Dear Mamma; in other words Dear Mrs. Mermet."

16. Paul Klee, *Tagebücher*, no. 425, 22 June 1902, p. 134; *The Diaries* (Berkeley: University of California Press, 1964), 124.

17. Quoted in Marcel Raymond, *De Baudelaire au surréalisme*, (Paris: Librairie José Corti, 1963), 275f.

18. André Gide, *Les Nourritures terrestres* (Paris: Gallimard, 1972), 19.

19. Regarding Robert Walser's indebtedness to *Jugendstil* see Irma Kellen-

berger, *Der Jugendstil und Robert Walser* (Bern: Francke, 1981). I have disagreed with her views in T. S. Evans, "'A Paul Klee in Prose': Design, Space, and Time in the Work of Robert Walser," *German Quarterly* 57 (1984): 32–34.

20. Werner Hofmann, *Von der Nachahmung zur Erfindung der Wirklichkeit: Die schöpferische Befreiung der Kunst, 1890–1917* (Cologne: DuMont Schauberg, 1970), 47.

21. Joseph Frank, *The Widening Gyre: Crisis and Mastery in Modern Literature* (Bloomington: Indiana University Press, 1968), 59.

22. Anna Balakian, *Literary Origins of Surrealism: A New Mysticism in French Poetry* (New York: New York University Press, 1965), 17.

23. Susan Sontag, "Walser's Voice," in Walser, *Selected Stories*, viii.

24. Cf. Franz Marc's diary entry on Christmas 1914, quoted in Peter Selz, *German Expressionist Painting* (Berkeley: University of California Press, 1968), 224: "I am beginning more and more to see behind, or, to put it better, through things, to see behind them something which they conceal, for the most part cunningly, with their outward appearance by hoodwinking man with a facade which is quite different from what it actually covers."

25. Hugo von Hofmannsthal, "Franz Stuck," in *Gesammelte Werke, Prosa I* (Frankfurt: S. Fischer, 1950), 197f.

26. In James Thrall Soby, *Giorgio de Chirico* (New York: Museum of Modern Art, 1955), 67.

27. Theo Elm, "Die Fiktion eines Entwicklungsromans: Zur Erzähl-Strategie in Peter Handkes Entwicklungsroman *Der kurze Brief zum langen Abschied*," in *Zu Peter Handke*, ed. Norbert Honsza (Stuttgart: Ernst Klett, 1982), 65, n. 34.

28. Robert Walser, *Geschwister Tanner*, in *Das Gesamtwerk* 4: 156; translation by the author.

29. Robert Walser, *Der Gehülfe*, in *Das Gesamtwerk* 5: 261; translation by the author.

30. Walser, *Der Gehülfe*, 96.

31. Paul Klee, "On Modern Art," in *The Thinking Eye*, ed. Jürg Spiller (New York: George Wittenborn, 1961), 92, 95.

32. Microscript 196, prose text 1, Zurich, Robert Walser Archive.

33. Robert Walser, "Ibsens Nora oder die Rösti," in *Das Gesamtwerk* 3: 354–55.

34. Cf. Paul Klee's definition of art in "Creative Credo," in *The Thinking Eye*, 80: "Learn to appreciate this *villégiature*: a change of air, and viewpoint, a world that distracts you, and gives you strength for the inevitable return to work-a-day grey."

### A Writer's Cache

1. The microscripts were part of Walser's literary estate, which became the property of his friend and executor, Carl Seelig, following Walser's death. The texts are written on 528 sheets of various sizes: 117 sheets are high-gloss printing paper; 158 sheets are from a Tusculum calendar for the year 1926; the remaining number is an assortment of papers ranging from

publishers' verifications of work printed or payment of honoraria, telegrams, and envelopes, to postcards and calling cards. The script, which incorporates a variety of abbreviations, is usually no more than two millimeters in height. With few exceptions, the texts are untitled, but individual texts are clearly distinguished by their spacing on the microscript sheet.

2. The approximate dating of the groups of microscripts is based primarily on Walser's references to specific texts in his correspondence as well as on the publication date of clean copies of microscript texts. There is evidence that Walser usually made his clean copies within days of the microscript original, although some of the material in the earlier manuscripts was used for submissions as late as the early thirties.

3. Presently included in Jochen Greven's expert thirteen-volume edition of Walser's works and letters under the title *Das Gesamtwerk* (1966–75), referred to as *GW*, is the prose Walser himself published in *Die Rose* (1925), prose that did not appear in book form, and unpublished clean-copy manuscripts in vol. 8 (*Olympia*). The final volume of works in Greven's edition also includes two important longer texts from the 117 sheets of high-gloss paper, *The "Felix" Scenes* (*GW* 12: 17–63) and the draft of Walser's last novel, *The Robber* (*GW* 12: 71–293). Beyond the 113 "new" prose texts, the texts on the high-gloss sheets also include 50 poems and some 20 works in dialogue form.

4. In this now often-cited prose text, first published in Greven's edition, Walser characterizes his prose works as follows: "In my own opinion, my prose pieces are nothing but parts of a long, plotless, realistic story. For me, the sketches I produce now and again are lesser or more comprehensive novel chapters. The novel I am still working on and adding to is ever the same and one might be able to designate it a variously cut up or disjoined first-person book" (*GW* 10: 323).

5. Quotations from microscript texts are cited according to Greven's numbering of the sheets on which the texts were written, corresponding to the physical sequence of the microscript sheets when they were made available to Greven in 1966. Small roman numerals refer to a text's occurence on a particular sheet. Translations fom the texts are in quotation marks.

6. The Bernese country pastor, novelist, and story writer Jeremias Gotthelf (1797–1854). Gotthelf, Gottfried Keller, and Conrad Ferdinand Meyer are counted Switzerland's most important writers in the nineteenth century.

7. Cf. Martin Walser, *Selbstbewusstsein und Ironie: Frankfurter Vorlesungen* (Frankfurt: Suhrkamp, 1981), especially chap. 3, "Einübung ins Nichts."

8. Franz Kafka, *Hochzeitsvorbereitungen auf dem Land* (*Wedding Preparations in the Country and Other Stories*, trans. Ernst Kaiser and Eithne Wilkins) (New York: Schocken Books, 1953), 343. Page reference is to German edition.

### Walser's Silence

1. Quoted from Christopher Middleton's "Postscript" in Robert Walser, *Selected Stories*, trans. Christopher Middleton and others with a foreword by Susan Sontag (New York: Farrar, Straus & Giroux, 1982), 193.

2. *Selected Stories*, 179–81. The German original is "Freiheitsaufsatz," in Robert Walser, *Das Gesamtwerk*, ed. Jochen Greven (Zurich and Frankfurt: Suhrkamp, 1978), 11: 200–3.

3. John Christopher Middleton, "Notizen eines Walser-Übersetzers," in *Über Robert Walser*, ed. Katharina Kerr (Frankfurt: Suhrkamp, 1978), 2: 73.

4. For her expert advice on the question of Walser's psychopathology I am greatly indebted to Dr. Johanna Mayer.

5. Following my lecture "Walser's Silence," Christopher Middleton contributed to the discussion with the remarks presented and edited in "A Parenthesis to the Discussion of Robert Walser's Schizophrenia" (see this volume). Elaborating on my emphasis on Walser's narcissism, he introduced Jungian and anthropological terminology—*puer aeternus* and *liminoid*—yet undermined these terms with references to Walser's "mystery" which "can not be 'boiled down' to anything" (p. 194). In my opinion, replacing one set of terms with another, whether psychological or anthropological, in the end falls short of Walser. His silence is Walser himself. It can be approached, but not reached by terms.

# Select Bibliography

## German Editions

*Das Gesamtwerk.* 13 vols. Ed. Jochen Greven. Geneva/Hamburg: Kossodo, 1966–75; Frankfurt: Suhrkamp, 1978.

## English Translations

*Jakob von Gunten.* Trans. and with an introduction by Christopher Middleton. Austin: University of Texas Press, 1969; New York: Vintage Books, 1983.

*Selected Stories.* Trans. Christopher Middleton and others, with a foreword by Susan Sontag. New York: Farrar, Straus & Giroux, 1982; Manchester: Carcanet, 1982; New York: Vintage Books, 1983.

"The Child." Trans. Mark Harman. In *Comparative Criticism,* ed. E. S. Shaffer, 261–64. Cambridge: Cambridge University Press, 1984.

"Prose." Trans. Christopher Middleton. *Texas Quarterly* 7, no. 3 (Fall 1964): 98–119.

"The Seamstress" and "Disaster." Trans. Herbert L. Kaufman. *Lyrik und Prosa* (Buffalo) 7, 1974.

## Critical Writings (English)

Avery, George C. *Inquiry and Testament: A Study of the Novels and Short Prose of Robert Walser.* Philadelphia: University of Pennsylvania Press, 1968.

———. "A Poet beyond the Pale: Some Notes on the Shorter Works of Robert Walser." *Modern Language Quarterly* 24, no. 2 (June 1963): 181–90.

Evans, Tamara S. "'A Paul Klee in Prose': Design, Space, and Time in the Work of Robert Walser." *German Quarterly* 57 (1984): 32–34.

Hamburger, Michael. "Explorers: Musil, Walser, Kafka." In *A Proliferation of Prophets,* 244–72. New York: St. Martin's Press, 1984.

Harman, Mark. "Stream of Consciousness and the Boundaries of Self-Conscious Fiction: The Works of Robert Walser." In *Comparative Criticism,* ed. E. S. Shaffer, 119–34. Cambridge: Cambridge University Press, 1984.

Middleton, J. C. "The Picture of Nobody: Some Remarks on Robert Walser with a Note on Walser and Kafka." *Revue des langues vivantes* 24 (1958): 404–28.

Parry, Idris. "The Writer as Servant." In *Hand to Mouth and Other Essays.* Manchester: Carcanet, 1981.

Unseld, Siegfried. "Robert Walser and His Publishers." In *The Author and His Publisher,* 191–273. Chicago: University of Chicago Press, 1980.

## Critical Writings (German)

Arnold, Heinz Ludwig, ed. *Robert Walser. Text und Kritik* 12/12a. March 1975. A collection of essays.

Camenzind-Herzog, Elisabeth. *Robert Walser: 'eine Art verlorener Sohn.'* Bonn: Bouvier, 1981.

Evans, Tamara S. "Von einem, der auszieht: Max Frisch in Sachen Robert Walser." *Monatshefte* (Wisconsin) 75, no. 4, Winter 1983.

Greven, Karl Joachim Wilhelm (Jochen). *Existenz, Welt und reines Sein im Werk Robert Walsers: Versuch zur Bestimmung von Grundstrukturen.* (Diss.) Cologne: W. Kleikamp, 1960.

Herzog, Urs. *Robert Walsers Poetik: Literatur und soziale' Entfremdung.* Tübingen: Niemeyer, 1974.

Jürgens, Martin. *Robert Walser: Die Krise der Darstellbarkeit.* Kronberg/ Taunus: Scriptor, 1973.

Kerr, Katharina, ed. *Über Robert Walser.* 3 vols. Frankfurt: Suhrkamp, 1978–79. A comprehensive collection of essays with an extensive bibliography.

Naguib, Nagi. *Robert Walser: Entwurf einer Bewusstseinsstruktur.* Berlin/ Munich: Fink, 1970.

Pulver, Elsbeth, and Arthur Zimmermann, eds. *Robert Walser.* Pro Helvetia series. Bern: Zytglogge, 1984.

## Biographical Works

Fröhlich, Elio, and Peter Hamm, eds. *Robert Walser: Leben und Werk in Daten und Bildern.* Frankfurt: Insel, 1980.

Mächler, Robert. *Das Leben Robert Walsers: Eine dokumentarische Biographie.* Frankfurt: Suhrkamp, 1976.

Seelig, Carl. *Wanderungen mit Robert Walser.* Frankfurt: Suhrkamp, 1978.

## Robert Walser as a Fictional Figure

Amann, Jürg. *Verirren oder das plötzliche Schweigen des Robert Walser.* Fischer novel series 5427, Frankfurt: Fischer, 1983.

Davenport, Guy. "A Field of Snow on a Slope of the Rosenberg." In *Da Vinci's Bicycle*, 149–85. Baltimore: Johns Hopkins Press, 1976.

Hofmann, Gert. "Der Austritt des Dichters Robert Walser aus dem Literarischen Verein." In *Gespräch über Balzacs Pferd: Vier Novellen.* Salzburg/ Vienna: Residenz, 1981.

Meyer, E. Y. "Ein grosser Spaziergänger." In *Die Hälfte der Erfahrung.* (Frankfurt: Suhrkamp, 1980).

# Notes on Contributors

**Walter Benjamin** (1892–1940). Critic and writer. Author of *Illuminations* (Harcourt, Brace, 1968), *Reflections* (Harcourt, Brace, 1978). Translation of "Robert Walser," in *Über Literatur* (Suhrkamp, 1975), 62–65.

**Elias Canetti.** Novelist, nonfiction writer, critic. Author of *Auto-da-Fé* (1946), *Crowds and Power* (1962), *Kafka's Other Trial* (1974). Nobel Prize for Literature, 1981. Contribution reprinted from *The Human Province*, trans. Joachim Neugroschel (Continuum, 1978), 228–30.

**Franz Kafka** (1883–1924). Letter reprinted from *Letters to Friends, Family, and Editors* (Schocken, 1977), 60–61.

**Robert Musil** (1880–1942). Author of *The Man without Qualities* (Coward-McCann, 1953). Translation of "Die Geschichten von Robert Walser," which originally appeared in *Die neue Rundschau* (Berlin) 2, no. 25 (1914): 167–69.

**Martin Walser.** West German novelist and playwright. Author of the novella *Runaway Horse* (Holt, Rinehart, 1980). Translation (slightly abridged) of "Über den Unerbittlichkeitsstil: Zum 100. Geburtstag von Robert Walser," in *Wer ist ein Schriftsteller? Aufsätze und Reden* (Suhrkamp, 1979), 67–93.

**Walter Arndt.** Sherman Fairchild Professor in the Humanities, Dartmouth College. Translator of Pushkin and Goethe among others.

**George Avery.** Professor of German, Swarthmore College. Author of a study of Robert Walser, *Inquiry and Testament* (University of Pennsylvania Press, 1968), and of numerous articles on German and Austrian authors.

**Susan Bernofsky.** A translator who lives and works in New Orleans.

**Tamara Evans.** Assistant Professor of German, Queens College, City University of New York. She is the author of a book on C. F. Meyer and of essays on Walser and other Swiss writers.

**Mark Harman.** Visiting Assistant Professor of German, Oberlin College. He has written a study of the literary affinity between Kleist and Kafka and essays on Kafka and Robert Walser.

**Winfried Kudszus.** Professor of German, University of California, Berkeley. Author of a study of Hölderlin and of numerous essays on Kafka, German Romanticism, and literature and psychopathology.

**Joseph McClinton.** A freelance translator who lives in Berkeley, California.

**Christopher Middleton.** Professor of German, University of Texas, Austin. Translator of Robert Walser and of other German writers. Author of five books of poetry.

**Tom Whalen.** A translator who lives and works in New Orleans.

# Acknowledgments

"Robert Walser" by Elias Canetti is from *The Human Province* by Elias Canetti, © 1978 the Continuum Publishing Company. Reprinted by permission.

The two drawings of Robert Walser by Guy Davenport are reprinted here by permission of the artist and *The Georgia Review*, © 1977 by the University of Georgia.

"Letter to Director Eisner" by Franz Kafka is reprinted by permission from *Letters to Friends, Family, and Editors*, edited by Max Brod, © 1977 Schocken Books, Inc.

"The *Stories* of Robert Walser" by Robert Musil is from *Gesammelte Werke* by Robert Musil, © 1978 by Rowohlt Verlag GmbH, Reinbek bei Hamburg. Reprinted by permission of Rowohlt Verlag Gmbh, Reinbek bei Hamburg.

"From Fantasy," "A Strange City," "A Genius," "Good Day, Giantess!," "Ovation," "Oskar," "An Address to a Button," "Jesus," "The Angel," "A Cigarette," "A Slap in the Face et cetera," "Letter to a Commissioner of Novellas," "For Zilch," "A Sketch," "A Little Landscape," "And Went," "Poem from the Microscripts," "Cinderella," and "Snowwhite" by Robert Walser are reprinted mit Genehmigung der Inhaberin der Rechte, der Carl Seelig-Stiftung Zürich Copyright Verlag Helmut Kossodo, Genf und Hamburg 1966, 1967, 1968, 1971, 1972. All rights reserved.

"Robert Walser" by Walter Benjamin is reprinted by permission aus "Über Literatur" © Suhrkamp Verlag Frankfurt am Main 1969.

"Unrelenting Style" by Martin Walser is reprinted by permission aus "Liebeserklärungen" © Suhrkamp Verlag Frankfurt am Main 1983.

# Index of Works by Robert Walser

# Index of Authors and Titles